NEW TESTA▮

EVERYDAY BIBLE STUDY SERIES

MARK

LIVING A JESUS-SHAPED LIFE

SCOT MCKNIGHT

QUESTIONS WRITTEN BY
BECKY CASTLE MILLER

Harper*Christian*
Resources

New Testament Everyday Bible Study Series: Mark
© 2023 by Scot McKnight

Requests for information should be addressed to:
HarperChristian Resources, 3900 Sparks Dr. SE, Grand Rapids, Michigan 49546

ISBN 978-0-310-12928-8 (softcover)
ISBN 978-0-310-12929-5 (ebook)

First Printing August 2023 / Printed in the United States of America

NEW TESTAMENT

EVERYDAY BIBLE STUDY SERIES

CONTENTS

For Northern MANT 2017

GENERAL
INTRODUCTION

Christians make a claim for the Bible not made of any other book. Or, since the Bible is a library shelf of many authors, it's a claim we make of no other shelf of books. We claim that God worked in each of the authors as they were writing so that what was scratched on papyrus expressed what God wanted communicated to the people of God. Which makes the New Testament (NT) a book unlike any other book. Which is why Christians are reading the NT almost two thousand years later with great delight. These books have the power to instruct us and to rebuke us and to correct us and to train us to walk with God every day. We read these books because God speaks to us in them.

Developing a routine of reading the Bible with an open heart, a receptive mind, and a flexible will is the why of the *New Testament Everyday Bible Studies*. But not every day will be the same. Some days we pause and take it in and other days we stop and repent and lament and open ourselves to God's restoring graces. No one word suffices for what the Bible does to us. In fact, the Bible's view of the Bible can be found by reading Psalm 119, the longest chapter in the Bible with 176 verses! It is a meditation on eight terms for what the Bible is and what the Bible does to those who listen to and read it. Its laws (*torah*) instruct us, its laws (*mishpat*) order us, its statutes direct us, its precepts inform us, its decrees guide us, its commands compel us, its words speak to us, and its promises comfort us, and it is no wonder that the author can sum all eight up as the "way" (119:3). Each of those terms still speaks to what happens when we open our minds to the Word of God.

Every day with the Bible then is new because our timeless and timely God communes with us in our daily lives in our world and in our time. Just as God spoke to Jesus in Galilee and Paul in Ephesus and John on Patmos. These various contexts help us hear God in our context so the *New Testament Everyday Bible Studies* will often delve into contexts. Most of us now have a Bible on our devices. We may well have several translations available to us everywhere we go every day. To hear those words we are summoned by God to open the Bible, to attune our hearts to God, and to listen to what God says. My prayer is that these daily study guides will help each of us become daily Bible readers attentive to the mind of God.

INTRODUCTION: READING THE GOSPEL OF MARK

The first four books of the New Testament are biographies of Jesus. Biographies tell the story about a person, in this Jesus. But they also do more, and the emphasis of this study guide will show how the story about Jesus shapes the pattern of discipleship. In particular, a Jesus-shaped discipleship conforms to the Jesus of the Cross into a cross-kind of discipleship. The Jesus of Mark is the One Crucified, but he is the Son of God, the Son of Man, the Son of David, and most especially he is the Messiah of Israel and the Lord of all. These terms, however, are swarmed by a narrative that takes Jesus throughout his public ministry in all its forms as well as constant opposition that comes to its end on a cross outside Jerusalem. All along the disciples are observing and learning what it means to be a follower of this kind of Jesus.

The Gospel of Mark is the shortest of the four. Mark's Gospel may have been the shortest, but the Second Gospel was the basis for both Matthew and Luke, who not only knew of Mark but copied from him, sometimes extensively. Mark sustains a fast-paced plot not only by compactness but also by using words suggesting the next event happened right away, immediately, and quickly some forty times. More than that, over half of the Gospel is about the last week. Mark, to put it succinctly, created a new kind of book: a biography of a new sort because the person is unlike any other person.

Like Matthew and Luke, Mark records the message from Jesus to be about God, about the kingdom of God, and about the people of the kingdom of God. In revealing his message, Jesus told parables aplenty, he did miracles all over the place, he gathered twelve special disciples, and he sent them on mission to spread the news. In that ministry of Jesus, he suffered constant resistance. I will explain this in the Study Guide, but a brief word is in order here. Jesus created rumors about what he was up to that reached the authorities in Galilee (Herod Antipas, Herodians), in Caesarea Maritima on the coast (Pontius Pilate), and in Jerusalem's temple authorities (Caiaphas, high priests, elders, teachers of the law [scribes], and the Pharisees). Like the apostle Paul who was sent to Damascus to silence the earliest Christians there, the temple authorities in Jerusalem sent the Pharisees and teachers of the law, joined at times with Herodians, to inspect Jesus to see if he was fomenting some kind of rebellion against the temple-state. Their concern ultimately was if the Roman authorities, from top down being Tiberius and Sejanus (his proxy emperor in Rome while Tiberius hung out on the island of Capri) and Pilate and Antipas, would be concerned enough to squash the movement of Jesus out of fear of a disruption.

The Gospel of Mark tells the story of Jesus interacting with the temple authorities from Galilee to Jerusalem. Along the way he is preparing disciples to follow him then and after his resurrection.

WORKS CITED IN THE STUDY GUIDE:

(Throughout the guide you will find the author's name and title, as noted in this list, with page numbers whenever I cite it):

Timothy G. Gombis, *Mark* (Grand Rapids: Zondervan, 2021). [Gombis, *Mark*]

Morna D. Hooker, *The Gospel according to Saint Mark* (Peabody, Massachusetts: Hendrickson, 1991). [Hooker, *Mark*]

Scot McKnight, *The Second Testament*, (Downers Grove: IVP, 2023). [McKnight, *The Second Testament*]

Emerson B. Powery, "The Gospel of Mark," in *True to Our Native Land*. (Minneapolis: Fortress Press, 2007). [Powery, "Mark"]

Bonnie Bowman Thurston, "The Gospel of Mark," in *The IVP Women's Bible Commentary* (ed. Catherine Clark Kroeger, Mary J. Evans; Downers Grove: IVP, 2002). [Thurston, "Mark"]

THE JESUS-SHAPED LIFE: A CROSS LIFE

Mark 8:27–9:1

²⁷ *Jesus and his disciples went on to the villages around Caesarea Philippi. On the way he asked them, "Who do people say I am?"*

²⁸ *They replied, "Some say John the Baptist; others say Elijah; and still others, one of the prophets."*

²⁹ *"But what about you?" he asked. "Who do you say I am?"*

Peter answered, "You are the Messiah."

³⁰ *Jesus warned them not to tell anyone about him.*

³¹ *He then began to teach them that the Son of Man must suffer many things and be rejected by the elders, the chief priests and the teachers of the law, and that he must be killed and after three days rise again.* ³² *He spoke plainly about this, and Peter took him aside and began to rebuke him.*

³³ *But when Jesus turned and looked at his disciples, he rebuked Peter. "Get behind me, Satan!" he said. "You do not have in mind the concerns of God, but merely human concerns."*

³⁴ *Then he called the crowd to him along with his disciples and said: "Whoever wants to be my disciple must deny themselves and take up their cross and follow me.* ³⁵ *For whoever wants to save their life will lose it, but whoever loses their life for me and for the gospel will save it.* ³⁶ *What good is it for someone to gain the whole*

world, yet forfeit their soul? [37] Or what can anyone give in exchange for their soul? [38] If anyone is ashamed of me and my words in this adulterous and sinful generation, the Son of Man will be ashamed of them when he comes in his Father's glory with the holy angels."

[9:1] And he said to them, "Truly I tell you, some who are standing here will not taste death before they see that the kingdom of God has come with power."

Special Note to the Reader: At the heart of discipleship in the Gospel of Mark is Mark 8:27–9:1, a passage that ties Jesus' life intimately to discipleship, so we begin in the first study with that passage. Mark has to be read from this central passage in order to understand how this Gospel works.

Mark constructs his biography of Jesus to tell the story about Jesus, but at the very same time he writes with disciples in mind. His central idea about discipleship is this: the life of Jesus shapes what the life of a follower of Jesus should look like. Or, to follow Jesus is to follow in the way of Jesus. First, Jesus is the Messiah. Second, he is a Messiah who will go to the cross but then be raised by the power of God. That means, third, following Jesus means a cross-shaped life that will also be followed by final victory. Jesus' cross-shaped life is the heart of what Mark tells us about Jesus, and the cross-shaped life is the heart of what he tells us about discipleship. Clear? Yes. Difficult? For sure.

Because these three themes are the heart and soul of the Gospel of Mark, we begin right in the middle of the Gospel of Mark, in a story-turning moment when the disciples will have first comprehended (if they did) that Jesus was going to be taken down by Jerusalem's authorities and when they were first instructed that their lives would need to conform to his life. In today's passage the cross-shaped lives of Jesus becomes a cross-shaped life for his followers.

A Beautiful Confession

It took eight chapters of Jesus' presence with the disciples before he could ask them one question and get the right answer. The question seems innocent enough, though it's not one any of us would ask in the way Jesus did. The question is, "Who do people say I am?" (8:27). He isn't curious. He's got a question that, when answered, leads to a more important question. They give a rough-and-ready straw poll. Some think Jesus is John the Baptist, now come back to life by the power of God; others think he's Elijah, who was expected to return to Israel before the arrival of the kingdom; others think Jesus is one of the prophets. That is, less likely one who had come back to life and more likely someone with the gift of a prophet.

His first question now answered, he asks the bigger one of two questions: "But what about you?" he asked. "Who do you say I am?" (8:29). Jews of Jesus' day had a general notion of the future coming Messiah, but their attention was more on getting Rome out of the land of Israel, welcoming an act of God that restored the people with conditions of the kingdom, and along with many—but not all—expected a king who could be called "Messiah." The common expectation for Messiah was a royal king who would lead Israel to victory over their enemies (Rome), liberate the people, and guide them into peace and joy. That's all at work when Peter says, "You are the Messiah" (8:29). With that confession of sorts, Peter and the others now examine the face of Jesus to see if he will affirm this breakthrough moment for Peter.

Jesus blunts that beautiful confession with the warning "not to tell anyone about him" (8:30). You would not be alone if you mutter under your breath, *But why?* Messiah means anointed king. King means kingdom. Kingdom means God is on the throne. Kingdom means peace and liberation. What's the problem here?

The problem is that the boilerplate view of "Messiah" was not what Jesus and his Father had in mind. What he says next not only shifts the Gospel of Mark, it also alters history and what it means to follow Jesus. The Jesus who will be followed will not be the Messiah of their expectation but a radically different kind of Messiah.

A SHOCKING FUTURE

The distinctive idea at the heart of the Christian faith is that its Messiah, its Savior, was crucified as a criminal on a Roman cross in front of the public of Jerusalem at a major high holiday, Passover. The apostle Paul will tell us that the central idea of a crucified Messiah was "a stumbling block to Jews and foolishness to Gentiles" (1 Corinthians 1:23). But what we take as an assumption no one in Jesus' world, especially in his inner circle of followers, considered possible. One thing Jews believed was that someday God would send the Messiah and the Messiah would be victorious over evil and enemies and would establish that Messiah on an eternal throne. They glued the word "Messiah" to "throne." Jesus melted the glue and glued the term "Messiah" to the term "cross." It was his most shocking idea. Crucifixion was a hideous display of violence, of retribution, and of public warning for any who chose rebellion against Rome.

Not only did Jesus predict rejection, he also prophesied to his followers that Jerusalem's leaders would be the agents of his rejection. In Mark 8:31 he pins the final rejection on the "elders, the chief priests and the teachers of the law."

What Jesus predicted could not be unpredicted, and what they heard could not be unheard. Even predicting that "after three days [he would] rise again" could not be heard because their minds were so shocked by a prediction of death. Jesus "spoke plainly," so plainly about his death that Peter "took him aside and began to rebuke" the Lord he was following! Jesus, knowing his mission, rebuked Peter right back and classified Peter's rebuke as "merely human concerns" that sound like "Satan," whose temptations are spelled out in Matthew and Luke (Matthew 4:1–11; Luke 4:1–13) but only briefly mentioned at Mark 1:12–13.

A Graphic Image

Jesus' prediction of a shocking, even confusing, future death for himself becomes a graphic image for discipleship. The first words for discipleship were "follow me" (1:17), and now both the "me" and the "follow" are sharpened in profile. The Me is the suffering Messiah, and the Follow is a cross-shaped life. Jesus' words deserve memorization: "Whoever wants to be my disciple must deny themselves and take up their cross and follow me" (8:34). A criminal who was to be crucified carried his own cross to the place of crucifixion. Crucifixion was connected in that day to "shame and disgrace" (Hooker, *Mark*, 209).

These words from my favorite writer, Dietrich Bonhoeffer, on discipleship re-express what Jesus told his disciples:

> Those who enter into discipleship enter into Jesus' death. They turn their living into dying; such has been the case from the very beginning. The cross is not the terrible end of a pious, happy life. Instead, it stands at the beginning of community with Jesus Christ. Whenever Christ calls us, his call leads us to death.
>
> But how should disciples know what their cross is? They will receive it when they begin to follow the suffering Lord. They will recognize their cross in communion with Jesus.
>
> Discipleship in essence never consists in a decision

for this or that specific action; it is always a decision for or against Jesus Christ (*Discipleship*, 87, 89, 202).

What does it mean to "take up their cross"? It means to live a *life of self-denial* for the redemption of others. It does not mean self-degradation, nor does it exclude healthy self-esteem. As Emerson Powery reminds us so clearly, nor does it mean "suffering for the sake of suffering" (Powery, "Mark," 138). The cross-life means *surrendering* our will and our agency to the ways of Jesus and the kingdom of God. It means *participating with all the others* who are on the path with Jesus. It means *self-discovery* of the cross-life for each individual person. Some *change callings or careers* to follow Jesus. Followers of Jesus *sacrifice* time and money and talent to follow Jesus. These words in italics are but a few of the many words one hears from followers of Jesus as they tell their experiences of following Jesus.

One can get trapped in self-denial to the point of self-harm if one stops with self-denial. Those who "lose" their former life in self-denial will actually "save" their life, and they will save their life by experiencing what Jesus himself experienced. As his death was overcome by resurrection, so our cross-life will be overcome when "the kingdom of God has come with power" (9:1). The cross-life of the way of Jesus is just as much a resurrection-life with Jesus. Defeat will be more than matched by a final eternal victory. The last word is neither self-denial nor death but life-affirmation. No, the last word is life, a life with God as God makes his home with us.

Questions for Reflection and Application

1. What are the three themes at the heart of Mark's Gospel?

2. How did Jesus subvert people's expectations of their Messiah?

3. What does it mean for following Jesus to be "cross-shaped"?

4. What are some denials or sacrifices you have had to make in following Jesus?

5. As you begin this study, answer Jesus' question to his disciples: Who do you say I am?

FOR FURTHER READING

Dietrich Bonhoeffer, *Discipleship* (Dietrich
Bonhoeffer Works; Minneapolis: Fortress, 2011).
Formerly called *The Cost of Discipleship*.

JESUS OF THE CROSS: ANNOUNCED AND BAPTIZED

Mark 1:1–13

¹ *The beginning of the good news about Jesus the Messiah, the Son of God,* ² *as it is written in Isaiah the prophet:*

> *"I will send my messenger ahead of you,*
> *who will prepare your way"—*
> ³ *"a voice of one calling in the wilderness,*
> *'Prepare the way for the Lord,*
> *make straight paths for him.' "*

⁴ *And so John the Baptist appeared in the wilderness, preaching a baptism of repentance for the forgiveness of sins.* ⁵ *The whole Judean countryside and all the people of Jerusalem went out to him. Confessing their sins, they were baptized by him in the Jordan River.* ⁶ *John wore clothing made of camel's hair, with a leather belt around his waist, and he ate locusts and wild honey.* ⁷ *And this was his message: "After me comes the one more powerful than I, the straps of whose sandals I am not worthy to stoop down and untie.* ⁸ *I baptize you with water, but he will baptize you with the Holy Spirit."*

⁹ *At that time Jesus came from Nazareth in Galilee and was baptized by John in the Jordan.* ¹⁰ *Just as Jesus was coming up out of the water, he saw heaven being torn open and the Spirit descending on him like a dove.* ¹¹ *And a voice came from heaven: "You are my Son, whom I love; with you I am well pleased."*

¹² *At once the Spirit sent him out into the wilderness,* ¹³ *and he was in the wilderness forty days, being tempted by Satan. He was with the wild animals, and angels attended him.*

Every paragraph in the Gospel of Mark is a special kind of biography of Jesus, and every paragraph is also about discipleship because discipleship in Mark is about the Jesus-shaped life. And the Jesus of the Gospel of Mark is the Jesus of the Cross, and that means a Jesus-shaped life is a cross-shaped life. But we don't follow Jesus in a wooden, copy-cat fashion. Rather, we observe Jesus in this Gospel and discern how the pattern of his life can shape our life.

Mark begins his Gospel with two notes that I want to sound here. First, he writes about the "beginning of the good news [the gospel] about Jesus the Messiah, the Son of God" (1:1). The gospel's origin occurs with the message preached by John the Baptist. There are good reasons to think the word "gospel" or "good news" here refers to the whole life of Jesus in this Gospel. In other words, the gospel itself is the story of the life of Jesus that brings into fulfillment the "good news" of Isaiah (cf, 40:9; 52:7; 60:6; 61:1). Mark quotes Isaiah 40:3 but take a look also at Malachi 3:1 where Elijah is in view, to make clear who this Messiah, Son of God, is. Jesus is preceded by "the messenger ahead of you, who will prepare your way," and his message prepares a path for the Messiah's arrival. The "messenger" in Mark's Gospel is John the Baptist, who matters only because he is a witness to Jesus, who matters most.

A closer look now at Isaiah 40, which records one of the Bible's greatest prophecies of the return of the Lord and the exiles to Jerusalem where they will experience the glory of God's beautiful redemption. The redemptive God is the "Sovereign LORD" (40:10), the "shepherd" (40:11), the "Holy One" (40:25), "everlasting" and the "Creator" (40:28), and before him the nations are but a "drop in a bucket" (40:15)– and this God is incomparable when the idols of the nations appear in the competition (40:18). This God revives the life of God's people. These names and ideas, and more beside them, are what readers of Mark 1:1–3 could have grasped.

The messenger sounds the second note, which turns our attention to John the Baptist and his baptism that prepares for the unique baptism of Jesus, at whose baptism the Father publicly announces his eternal approval. Jesus' baptism anticipates the cross.

THE BAPTIST

John is a relative of Jesus. His ministry involved three dimensions: (1) he was in the very wilderness that evoked the arrival of the children of Israel from Egypt and the return of exiles to Jerusalem (Isaiah 40 again), (2) he preached "a baptism of repentance for the forgiveness of sins" (1:4), and (3) he administered a dipping or dunking of the repentant into the Jordan River, the very river that had been crossed to enter into the Land. One could call John's ministry, and I mean no irreverence here, "street theater." He wanted people to perceive that as God had led his people into the Land in the past, so he was doing it all over again with the baptized.

Three words are combined: baptism, repentance, and forgiveness (of sins). The baptism is an act of repentance, which means a complete turning around (conversion), and when baptism and repentance combine, they result in forgiveness. We may be tempted to diminish the act of baptism as secondary to the inner work of repentance, but we would fail a first century Jewish worldview if we did. Ritual action and repentance blended into one another for such persons. Neither the ritual alone nor repentance alone led to forgiveness because it was next to impossible for a first century Jew to think of repentance without a ritual. If you were to ask a Galilean follower of Jesus *When did you discover forgiveness?*, that person would have answered, *I was baptized just after Passover* (or some such event on the calendar).

John was a bit weird. Fred Craddock puts it this way: "He was not a beautiful candle burning softly in the sanctuary. He was a prairie fire, the very fire of God scorching the earth. He was no diplomat trying to make yes sound like no and no sound like yes to please everybody. He just said, 'The Judge is coming and I'm here to serve subpoenas'" (Craddock, *Collected Sermons*, 111). The Baptist's clothing and diet was part of his gig, his street theater performance of a new beginning for the new people of God. He looked like a rigorous, disciplined, ascetic prophet, like Elijah (2 Kings 1:8), who was living off the Land as an act of fasting and grief over the condition of Judea.

The Gospel of Mark now adds a fourth dimension to the three above: (4) the center of his preaching was not baptism but Jesus (1:7–8). What he told the crowds who came to his baptism was announced in a most public place because it was along the route down the Jordan valley on which many traveled on their way to Jerusalem. His message was about Jesus, that he was "more powerful (or stronger) than I," and John's status compared to Jesus' was that of a slave or servant who untied the straps of a master's sandals (1:7). What's more, the watery baptism of John is outstripped by the Holy-Spirit-y baptism of Jesus (1:8).

And with John's explanation of the fourth dimension of his ministry the camera shifts from John to Jesus and the rest of this Gospel will be about Jesus.

THE SON

Jesus undergoes John's baptism, which was a baptism of repentance for the forgiveness of sins. If you think, as I do, that Jesus was sinless, we need to adjust what Jesus was doing when compared with others. One of the best explanations is that Jesus vicariously repents for us, or at least, enters into the water to identify himself with sinners who need forgiveness. I like how Barbara Brown Taylor sketches the scene, reminding us that we are the ones exposed by our nervousness about what Jesus was doing when he got in line with sinners for baptism:

> You see the problem. We spend a lot of time in the Christian church talking about God's love for sinners, but we sure do go to a lot of trouble not to be mistaken for one of them. Guilt by association and all that. Only Jesus—our leader and our Lord—did not seem too concerned about that. In him, God's being-with-us included God's being in the river with us, in the flesh with us, in the sorrow of repentance and the joy of new life with us. So what if he did not have anything of his own to be sorry about? (*Home By Another Way*, 35).

In his baptism, Jesus officially begins his crucifixion. Not only is his baptism unique, but what happens next makes Jesus one-of-a-kind.

When he ascends out of the water, a cosmic sign occurs: The Spirit descends on him "like a dove" (1:10), a

Pentecost-like anointing of Jesus for his mission and ministry. Accompanying the cosmic sign, a cosmic voice, the Father's, publicly identifies *who Jesus is:* My Son, the Son the Father loves, and the loved Son in whom God the Father is delighted (1:11). The term "Son" identifies Jesus as the royal Son (Psalm 2:7; Isaiah 42:1), the Davidic Messiah, the One the Father sends into the world to redeem the world, the One empowered by the Spirit to accomplish everything we are about to read in this Gospel. He is the Son, too, who will be crucified and raised.

The baptized and publicly announced and affirmed Son is driven by that empowering Spirit "out into the wilderness" to be tempted. As those Israelites went through the baptism of the Red Sea (without getting wet, of course) into the wilderness, so Jesus' baptism leads to the wilderness. That is, he will undergo in forty days what the children of Israel underwent in forty years. He will be tested "by Satan" in order to establish a sinless Son of God who can lead a new people into the way of the kingdom.

Followers of Jesus begin their following when they enter into the water to be baptized in the baptism of Jesus, and into the wilderness of tempting with Jesus ahead of them, alongside them, under them, behind them, and above them. And some angels unawares with us, and perhaps too some "wild animals"! The latter refers to the wildness of the wilderness.

QUESTIONS FOR REFLECTION AND APPLICATION

1. What is the gospel as defined in this section?

2. How did ritual action and repentance work together for first century Jews?

3. What role did John the Baptist play in Jesus' ministry?

4. As you observe Jesus in Mark, what are some ways you discern that the pattern of his life can shape your life?

5. If you have been baptized, what was your experience of entering into following Jesus? If you have not been baptized, is that something you would consider doing?

FOR FURTHER READING

Fred Craddock, *The Collected Sermons of Fred B. Craddock* (Louisville: Westminster John Knox, 2011).
Barbara Brown Taylor, *Home By Another Way* (Lanham, MD: Rowman and Littlefield, 1999).

JESUS OF THE CROSS: FOLLOWING

Mark 1:14–20

14 After John was put in prison, Jesus went into Galilee, proclaiming the good news of God. 15 "The time has come," he said. "The kingdom of God has come near. Repent and believe the good news!"

16 As Jesus walked beside the Sea of Galilee, he saw Simon and his brother Andrew casting a net into the lake, for they were fishermen. 17 "Come, follow me," Jesus said, "and I will send you out to fish for people." 18 At once they left their nets and followed him.

19 When he had gone a little farther, he saw James son of Zebedee and his brother John in a boat, preparing their nets. 20 Without delay he called them, and they left their father Zebedee in the boat with the hired men and followed him.

The opening clause of today's passage is ominous. "After John was put in prison" harbors a dark secret that Jesus will also be hauled in by the authorities. The ominous rippled out to the disciples too. So in today's passage the Jesus who will be of the Cross calls four men to drop what they're doing and join him on the Cross-road to the kingdom of God. They are called to a Jesus-shaped life.

Message in
Seven Words

Jesus picked special words to articulate his message. First, he says the *time* has been filled out, that is, the plan of God in history has run its course. Second, the *"kingdom of God has come near"* (1:15). The plan of God is for the kingdom of God, and the kingdom of God is what is looming on the horizon. Jesus' most significant term for his mission and ministry is *kingdom*. It is (1) God's kingdom because God is the king and that means the kingdom is not Herod's or Tiberius'; (2) God's kingdom enters history both in redeeming or saving, and by then governing; (3) God's kingdom requires there be a coalition of people, and in the Old Testament it is Israel and then it expands to be the people of Jesus; (4) for God to redeem and rule a people, God provides instruction, law, or a way of life (the teachings of Jesus); and (5) everywhere the term "kingdom" is used in the Jewish world, kingdom requires a territory. Of course, readers of the Bible know all about the Land of Israel but in the early church "land" started to expand and grow into "world." The land promise thus grows under the kingdom vision of Jesus.

What Jesus preaches is that this five-fold sense of kingdom has been launched, has been started, has been set in motion by Jesus in the power of the Spirit. But that kingdom takes root in the life of someone if the person *repents* and *believes* in the *good news* about who Jesus is (see Mark 1:11) and embraces his mission. To repent is to admit our wrongs and sins, to confess them before God, and to surrender ourselves to God to walk in the way of Jesus. And to believe in the good news is to trust that Jesus is the Agent of God's now-launched kingdom.

MISSION IN FOUR LIVES

Jesus' mission is aimed at individual persons turning their lives over to him in order to participate in a coalition of people called "kingdom." To repent and to believe in the good news about Jesus and the kingdom now finds concrete illustrations in two sets of brothers: Simon (Peter) and Andrew as well as James and John, two sons of a man named Zebedee (1:16–20). Each of the four is a fisherman in the Sea of Galilee, which was filled with tilapia, and today that fish is called "St. Peter's Fish" in the restaurants of the Holy Land. Jesus' words for them are "Follow me." Added to the act of following Jesus was a mission statement: I will turn your fishing for fish into fishing for humans, that is, to evangelize and mentor others into joining the kingdom coalition.

We learn much about Peter and John in the pages of the New Testament, both good and bad, but we don't learn much about either Andrew or James. But each of their lives illustrates in differing ways what it means to repent, to believe, and to follow Jesus into a Jesus-shaped life. Jesus' calling arrests the brothers, captures their imaginations of what life can be like, they drop all they are doing, and they begin to accompany Jesus because they embrace who he is and his kingdom. To follow is to walk with, to listen to, to observe, and to live like Jesus. All four of these men seem to give up their careers of fishing to be with Jesus.

QUESTIONS FOR REFLECTION
AND APPLICATION

1. What are five important points about the meaning of kingdom to Jesus?

2. What does the "territory" aspect of kingdom mean for Christians in the book of Acts and onward?

3. What were the jobs in the kingdom to which Jesus called Peter, Andrew, James, and John?

4. How has following Jesus re-shaped your career ambitions or lifestyle?

5. What do you perceive to be your role in the kingdom?

JESUS OF THE CROSS: POWER AND POPULARITY

Mark 1:21–45

Cosmic Power

²¹ *They went to Capernaum, and when the Sabbath came, Jesus went into the synagogue and began to teach.* ²² *The people were amazed at his teaching, because he taught them as one who had authority, not as the teachers of the law.* ²³ *Just then a man in their synagogue who was possessed by an impure spirit cried out,* ²⁴ *"What do you want with us, Jesus of Nazareth? Have you come to destroy us? I know who you are—the Holy One of God!"*

²⁵ *"Be quiet!" said Jesus sternly. "Come out of him!"* ²⁶ *The impure spirit shook the man violently and came out of him with a shriek.*

²⁷ *The people were all so amazed that they asked each other, "What is this? A new teaching—and with authority! He even gives orders to impure spirits and they obey him."* ²⁸ **News about him spread quickly over the whole region of Galilee.**

Healing and Cosmic Power

²⁹ *As soon as they left the synagogue, they went with James and John to the home of Simon and Andrew.* ³⁰ *Simon's mother-in-law was in bed with a fever, and they immediately told Jesus about her.*

³¹ So he went to her, took her hand and helped her up. The fever left her and she began to wait on them.

³² That evening after sunset the people brought to Jesus all the sick and demon-possessed. ³³ The whole town gathered at the door, ³⁴ and Jesus healed many who had various diseases. He also drove out many demons, but he would not let the demons speak because they knew who he was.

*³⁵ **Very early in the morning, while it was still dark, Jesus got up, left the house and went off to a solitary place, where he prayed. ³⁶ Simon and his companions went to look for him, ³⁷ and when they found him, they exclaimed: "Everyone is looking for you!" ³⁸ Jesus replied, "Let us go somewhere else— to the nearby villages—so I can preach there also. That is why I have come." ³⁹ So he traveled throughout Galilee, preaching in their synagogues and driving out demons.***

Healing Power

⁴⁰ A man with leprosy came to him and begged him on his knees, "If you are willing, you can make me clean."

⁴¹ Jesus was indignant. He reached out his hand and touched the man. "I am willing," he said. "Be clean!" ⁴² Immediately the leprosy left him and he was cleansed.

*⁴³ Jesus sent him away at once with a strong warning: ⁴⁴ "See that you don't tell this to anyone. But go, show yourself to the priest and offer the sacrifices that Moses commanded for your cleansing, as a testimony to them." ⁴⁵ Instead he went out and began to talk freely, spreading the news. **As a result, Jesus could no longer enter a town openly but stayed outside in lonely places. Yet the people still came to him from everywhere.***

Mark opens his account of the public ministry of Jesus with a series of stories about the Spirit's power at work in and through Jesus. Today's passage reports on Jesus' various power encounters followed (in bold) the spreading of this news. The stories are about *Jesus'* power. All eyes are drawn to Jesus, and the stories set up the second chapter of this Gospel where opposition to Jesus begins to appear.

THE POWER OF JESUS

Eric Clapton, in his song *Change the World*, crooned "If I can reach the stars . . . If I could be king," and over and over, "If I could change the world." Jesus had far more power than Eric Clapton, and he launched the redemption of the world, one-by-one. The Bible, untouched and unstained by Enlightenment's and scientism's reduction of all that matters to the material, both believes and experiences spiritual powers at work in this world. These powers encounter Jesus, and he defeats their evil.

First, Jesus' teachings in the synagogue in Capernaum are so impressive "the people were amazed at his teaching" and "authority" (1:21–22). So impressive in fact that a man with a contaminating spirit (NIV has "possessed by"), which made him spiritually unclean and a social contaminant, blurts out questions that identify both Jesus' mission to conquer the evil powers at work and it identifies Jesus as "the Holy One of God" (1:23–24). Other than the Father who identified Jesus, and John who heard the Father, the next to recognize Jesus for *who he really was* is a man gripped by demons. Spiritual power sent from God encounters spiritual power in the grip of the devil. By the power of his presence and word, Jesus expels the "impure spirit" from a shaking, shrieking man. Physical symptoms of a spirit's last-ditch effort as well as of a spiritual victory.

Second, there is a large, lakeside home just south of the synagogue in Capernaum that has been assigned to Peter for a long time. Many think the third century decision to build a church on top of it, which was destroyed by an earthquake a few centuries later, indicates that this was Peter's home. A

Catholic church rests over the still-visible remains of Peter's home.* In that home, the evening after exorcising the demon in the synagogue, Jesus heals Peter's mother-in-law of a "fever" (1:30–31). Healed, she returns to a traditional, customary role as matron of the house and serves them.

Third, news about Jesus' exorcism and a healing spread. That evening everyone with a sickness showed up at the door for healing, and Mark with a little hyperbole, says "the whole town gathered at the door" to Peter's home. Of course. So Jesus becomes the local healer of "various diseases" and exorcist of "many demons," on which he put a gag order (1:33–34). He silenced them because he didn't want them to be the ones who identified him. He wanted the Father and his followers to have that task.

The fourth act of Jesus' healing powers figuratively scrapes a man clean of his leprosy, which was a general term in the New Testament for someone who had an eruption of the skin. Not all that is called "leprosy" in the Gospels refers to the very serious Hansen's disease. This helps explain why some persons with leprosy mixed with society while others, Luke 17:11–19 for example, did not. Leprosy ends when Jesus makes the man "clean" (Mark 1:40–42), which shows that the disease makes a person unclean and therefore unfit for some activities, especially entrance into the temple in Jerusalem. So Jesus makes him fit for the temple and instructs him to go to one of Jerusalem's priests, offer the appropriate sacrifice (Leviticus 14) for his "cleansing" and as a witness to the priests (Mark 1:44). Just what his witness was is our guess, but one could argue it was so the priests would learn Jesus could heal people from leprosy.

---

* "The House of Peter: The Home of Jesus in Capernaum?", Biblical Archaeology Society, October 13, 2022, https://www.biblicalarchaeology.org/daily/biblical-sites-places/biblical-archaeology-sites/the-house-of-peter-the-home-of-jesus-in-capernaum/

THE POPULARITY OF JESUS

No one in any small corner of the globe would be surprised that Jesus' name became known and his powers circulated into a swirling hope of healing for anyone with a sickness. Notice that each section in today's passage (as printed above) ends in bolded words indicating growing popularity for Jesus. Notice there's some progression here:

1. The people are amazed at his teaching and powers (1:22, 27).
2. News spreads "over the whole region of Galilee" (1:28).
3. People bring the sick and the "whole town" gathers (1:32, 33).
4. Jesus withdraws, but his disciples tell him "everyone is looking for you!" (1:37).
5. So Jesus leaves Capernaum and goes "through Galilee" where he preaches in synagogues and exorcises demons (1:39).
6. The man healed of leprosy, instead of hauling down to Jerusalem, chooses to "talk freely" (a kind of social media blast) (1:45).
7. The result is that "Jesus could no longer enter a town openly" and needs to withdraw into wilderness places (NIV: "lonely places" at 1:45; the term "wilderness" deserves to be more explicit because of its connections to 1:4, 13).
8. The people still find him (1:45).

Jesus is not seeking power, fame, nor celebrity. Because those are not his motives, this popularity theme deserves special notice. We can locate ourselves among the throngs of people both impressed by Jesus and wondering who he might be. Not only do we locate ourselves among them, we take a step out of the masses to hold hands with the disciples of Jesus. Still enthralled with his power and popularity, we perceive Jesus as king, as Lord, and as Savior who calls us to follow him.

Something about this Jesus we follow transforms as we read pages of the story of Jesus. Mark begins already in the first chapter to describe the opening phase of the *conflict in Galilee* between Jesus and his followers, on the one hand, and the temple authorities and Pharisees, on the other hand. Both want to persuade the ordinary people of Galilee. Various words for the people occur hundreds of times in the Gospels. So, we begin here to observe how important the crowds and people and populace become to the two sides of the conflict. Jesus wants them, has strategies to persuade them, but the Pharisees and the temple authorities have them in their grip until Jesus shows up. The populace's accumulating presence around Jesus sets the stage for the powers rejecting Jesus and eventually for his crucifixion. The Jesus of the Cross then is a Jesus whose mission was to gather the people under the wings of redemption.

This story told by Calvin Miller aptly points to where this popularity theme will land and where it has resonance in the history of one institution:

I happened to be at Columbia International University in South Carolina. I was passing through the hall-ways when I came into a large room of that school. In this room I noticed that its walls were covered with pictures of men and women. One of the university students happened to pass the room at the very moment I stood surveying those pictures. "Are these pictures of your past presidents?" I asked. "Presidents!" he almost shouted, as though I had insulted him. "Hardly presidents. These are the important people who have graduated from this school. Every picture in this room is not just a graduate but a martyr." . . . "You mean every person pictured here actually died for Jesus in some part of the world under some kind of persecution?" "That's exactly what I mean. Go read the tags." I did. Beside each picture was a tiny tag that told where the person had died and what was the price they had paid for their service. "This is remarkable," I said. I thought of the new picture recently hung in our rotunda. "At our school we put up pictures of our presidents." "Presidents! At our school we put up pictures of our martyrs." (Miller, *Life is Mostly Edges*, 351–352).

Like the Gospel of Mark's portrait of Jesus.

QUESTIONS FOR REFLECTION AND APPLICATION

1. Why did Jesus silence the demons and the people he freed from demonic power?

2. What do Jesus' healings of possessed people and diseased people have in common?

3. How does Jesus' celebrity status progress throughout this passage and the Gospel of Mark as a whole?

4. How does Mark set up the conflict of his narrative in the first chapter?

5. If you had the chance to see Jesus in person in Galilee, what would you have asked him to do for you?

FOR FURTHER READING

Eric Clapton, "Change the World," Source: *Musixmatch*. Songwriters: Wayne Kirkpatrick / Tommy L. Sims / Gordon Scott Kennedy. Change the World lyrics © Universal Music Corp., Universal Music—Brentwood Benson Songs, Sondance Kid Music, Downtown Dmp Songs, Universal Polygram Int. Publishing Inc., Universal Music—Brentwood Benson Publications.

Calvin Miller, *Life is Mostly Edges: A Memoir* (Nashville: Thomas Nelson, 2010).

JESUS OF THE CROSS: CONFLICT

Mark 2:1–3:6

^{1} A few days later, when Jesus again entered Capernaum, the people heard that he had come home. ^{2} They gathered in such large numbers that there was no room left, not even outside the door, and he preached the word to them. ^{3} Some men came, bringing to him a paralyzed man, carried by four of them. ^{4} Since they could not get him to Jesus because of the crowd, they made an opening in the roof above Jesus by digging through it and then lowered the mat the man was lying on. ^{5} When Jesus saw their faith, he said to the paralyzed man, "Son, your sins are forgiven."

^{6} Now some teachers of the law were sitting there, thinking to themselves, ^{7} "Why does this fellow talk like that? He's blaspheming! Who can forgive sins but God alone?"

^{8} Immediately Jesus knew in his spirit that this was what they were thinking in their hearts, and he said to them, "Why are you thinking these things? ^{9} Which is easier: to say to this paralyzed man, 'Your sins are forgiven,' or to say, 'Get up, take your mat and walk'? ^{10} But I want you to know that the Son of Man has authority on earth to forgive sins." So he said to the man, ^{11} "I tell you, get up, take your mat and go home." ^{12} He got up, took his mat and walked out in full view of them all. This *amazed everyone and they praised God, saying, "We have never seen anything like this!"*

13 Once again Jesus went out beside the lake. A large crowd came to him, and he began to teach them. 14 As he walked along, he saw Levi son of Alphaeus sitting at the tax collector's booth. "Follow me," Jesus told him, and Levi got up and followed him.

15 While Jesus was having dinner at Levi's house, many tax collectors and sinners were eating with him and his disciples, for there were many who followed him. 16 When the teachers of the law who were Pharisees saw him eating with the sinners and tax collectors, they asked his disciples: "Why does he eat with tax collectors and sinners?"

17 On hearing this, Jesus said to them, "It is not the healthy who need a doctor, but the sick. I have not come to call the righteous, but sinners."

18 Now John's disciples and the Pharisees were fasting. Some people came and asked Jesus, "How is it that John's disciples and the disciples of the Pharisees are fasting, but yours are not?"

19 Jesus answered, "How can the guests of the bridegroom fast while he is with them? They cannot, so long as they have him with them. 20 But the time will come when the bridegroom will be taken from them, and on that day they will fast.

21 "No one sews a patch of unshrunk cloth on an old garment. Otherwise, the new piece will pull away from the old, making the tear worse. 22 And no one pours new wine into old wineskins. Otherwise, the wine will burst the skins, and both the wine and the wineskins will be ruined. No, they pour new wine into new wineskins."

23 One Sabbath Jesus was going through the grainfields, and as his disciples walked along, they began to pick some heads of grain. 24 The Pharisees said to him, "Look, why are they doing what is unlawful on the Sabbath?"

25 He answered, "Have you never read what David did when he and his companions were hungry and in need? 26 In the days of Abiathar the high priest, he entered the house of God and ate the consecrated bread, which is lawful only for priests to eat. And he also gave some to his companions."

²⁷ Then he said to them, "The Sabbath was made for man, not man for the Sabbath. ²⁸ So the Son of Man is Lord even of the Sabbath."

³:¹ Another time Jesus went into the synagogue, and a man with a shriveled hand was there. ² Some of them were looking for a reason to accuse Jesus, so they watched him closely to see if he would heal him on the Sabbath. ³ Jesus said to the man with the shriveled hand, "Stand up in front of everyone."

⁴ Then Jesus asked them, "Which is lawful on the Sabbath: to do good or to do evil, to save life or to kill?" But they remained silent.

⁵ He looked around at them in anger and, deeply distressed at their stubborn hearts, said to the man, "Stretch out your hand." He stretched it out, and his hand was completely restored. ⁶ Then the Pharisees went out and began to plot with the Herodians how they might kill Jesus.

We have emerged from the throngs of people impressed by Jesus to join those who follow Jesus, and in Mark 2 we will observe the formation of an intense reaction to Jesus that leads to his utter rejection. This, too, matters for those who want to embrace the Jesus of the Cross. There are five separable events in this passage: healing, calling Levi and eating with sketchy persons, a query about his fasting practices, an accusation about working on the Sabbath, and another Sabbath day healing. Three themes are present in all five events. Other themes could be brought to the surface, too, including what God is like in today's passage.

THE WATCHING CROWDS

Once again, let's notice the popularity of Jesus in today's passage. Again in Capernaum a big crowd assembles around

Jesus (2:2, 4), he heals a man, and "this amazed everyone" (2:12). Along the massive lake a "large crowd" gathers, out of which he calls Levi to follow him (2:13–14), leading to a meal with "many" at Levi's house (2:15). You may notice one more use of "people," the one found at 2:18. However, the Greek text has no such word and all we have is "*they* come and say to him." Instead of this being "people," as we have seen already so many times, the ones with questions are "John's disciples and the Pharisees" (2:18). But, grabbing the attention of the "teachers of the law" (2:6) and now the "Pharisees" (2:18) reveals how widespread the attraction of Jesus has become.

THE POWERFUL LORD

As in Mark's first chapter, so in today's passage: *Jesus does astounding miracles.* One event after another leads to redemption. He pronounces a paralyzed man's sins forgiven and heals him to reveal his power (2:3, 5, 10–12). Morna Hooker rightly observes that "there is nothing in Jewish literature to suggest that any man—not even a messiah—would have the authority to forgive sins" (Hooker, *Mark*, 88). He converts a tax collector and attracts both those considered "sinners," which would mean anyone from law non-observant to those who flout their disobedience, and "tax collectors," which means Jesus has worked redemption among those least likely to be amenable to the ways of the law (2:13–15). Jesus justifies himself with "I have not come to call the righteous, but sinners," and both righteous and sinners could have scare quotes around them (2:17).

He's not done: when asked about fasting he makes the bold claim that as long as he, the bridegroom, is with them, it's time to celebrate and not fast (2:18–22). When some of the law observant people voice their opinion that Jesus' disciples grabbing heads of grain and eating their seeds violates the law not to work on the Sabbath, Jesus claims he is "Lord even of the Sabbath" (2:23–27). And, finally, the long section we are considering comes to a climactic moment when Jesus heals a man with a "shriveled hand," again on the Sabbath, and apparently it is the Pharisees who find his Sabbath observance lacking (3:1–6).

Jesus has a heart for those with various disabilities, knowing that such a category as "disabled" itself dishonors a person's integrity and viability and social fit. However we classify such persons, Jesus' approach is to restore them out of such social labeling and to reveal to all that all are loved by God and fit for the kingdom. Louise Gosbel, a professor in Australia, helps us to define what disability means. She writes, "it is not simply that an individual lives with a particular health condition or impairment, but it is also the resultant impact this condition has on an individual's ability to function within society, including any experience or marginalization or stigmatization associated with the health condition or impairment" (Gosbel, "Disability," 228). Tim Gombis points his finger at church-y exclusiveness with this question, "Why is [Jesus 'eating with all the wrong people'], running the risk of being seen to endorse them, *when you order your community habits to ensure you never run into them?*" (Gombis, *Mark*, 86).

Popularity of Jesus as a power-working Lord in Mark 2 does not stand out from what we read in Mark's first chapter. What does stand out is the clear and pervasive opposition to seemingly everything he's doing. Which is hyperbole, of course, but exaggeration of a reality remains a reality, to which we now turn.

THE PLOTTING CRITICS

Some of the criticisms of Jesus strike many as churlish. Who's against healing a paralyzed man or a man with a shriveled hand? And why would someone oppose such redemptive moments by appealing to a law? Not many, and that's probably where we are safest. Not many Jewish leaders and not many Jews would be against what Jesus was doing. So we need to explain these criticisms better than thinking all Jews were like this or that all Pharisees were like this. Those would both be false. Here's my explanation. The power in Galilee and Judea is anchored in Rome. In Judea we need to think of Pontius Pilate and the high priest, Caiaphas. In Galilee, we need to think of Herod Antipas. A very important element of the leaders' conflict with Jesus was the utter demand from Rome, which was ruled at this time by Tiberius who was ruling from the island of Capri through the conniving Sejanus, to keep the peace and to avoid populist/populace riots and rebellions. Jerusalem was run by priests. The temple authorities have sent the Pharisees to Galilee, where they will have needed support from Herod Antipas (the "Herodians" in the Gospels), because they've heard of stories about Jesus, and the temple leaders want a report on what's going on. They are confident in the compelling voice of the Pharisees because they were the first century leaders of the populace of both Judea and Galilee. Do you know the name "Nicodemus" from the Gospel of John's third chapter? Do you know that his name means *conqueror of the people*? One has to wonder if it was a nickname for other Pharisees.

Here's the download for reading this section in Mark:

1. the Pharisees and teachers of the law are a united front
2. *sent by the temple authorities*
3. to get things in order in Galilee.

The Pharisees, then, are temple agents with a mission to maintain their own popularity and silence voices that could disrupt the peace and status quo. The fear of the temple agents was singular: riots that could bring down the wrath of the Roman power, either Pilate or Antipas. They know Jesus' popularity creates concern of the crowds shifting from the temple agents and Pharisees to Jesus, and if that happens the power shifting could create a social disturbance.

As you read the next few paragraphs, locate yourself with the disciples of Jesus. Ask yourself what they had to be asking, even in the glow of their love for Jesus: *What could happen to us if we stick with Jesus?* What does a Jesus-shaped life look like?

The accusations of the temple agents begin with the "teachers of the law" (or scribes). The first allegation is that Jesus claims to do what only God can do: forgive sins (2:6–7). Jesus heals the man, proving the power of God at work in him, and the people side with Jesus (2:12). The second accusation comes from "teachers of the law who were Pharisees" (2:15–16). Jesus eats with those they consider outcasts, and Jesus responds by claiming his mission is for the "sinners" (2:17). Emerson Powery points to a movie, which I remember from my childhood, that was as justice-shaping as it was provocative for many. The movie was *Guess Who's Coming to Dinner*. The actor was the African American Sidney Poitier and the offended were white folks (Powery, "Mark," 125). Like Jesus, many Christians actively reach out to the marginalized of our day in order to follow Jesus' inclusive compassion for all. Jesus' eating with these folks embodies a reworking of God's grace and castigates the social exclusionary forces of how some frame their religious practices. That Jesus' message at the table led such persons out of their sinful ways would have been embraced by all Jewish leaders.

The third is more of a question that insinuates Jesus is off base on his fasting practice. The question comes from the Baptist's own followers as well as from the temple agents, the

Pharisees. They want to know why he doesn't fast as they do. His typical silencing answer clarifies that the kingdom has been launched. Fasting therefore can cease *as long as* he is with them. (Did anyone in that day catch the time limitation for Jesus?) It's time to celebrate. It's time to let the kingdom's power explode into kingdom ways, including the demolition of sexism, racism, and classism.

The fourth allegation comes from the Pharisees again. They query Jesus' followers for harvesting on the Sabbath, and Jesus justifies their actions by connecting himself and his followers to David, which may have surprised the Pharisees. What did surprise, even stun, them was the claim that he, the "Son of Man," is the Lord over the Sabbath (2:28). The claim is beyond stunning. Jesus, the Son of Man of Daniel 7? Really. Whether they thought of Daniel 7 is disputable since "son of man" could have meant little more than "a human" who represents all humans. What is not disputable is what is meant by "Lord of the Sabbath." The claim is that he can decide what constitutes divinely approved behavior on the Sabbath. Furthermore, he wants them to perceive that the Sabbath is a day for not working, for relaxation, for family and joy and fun. For gathering with friends. For avoiding all labor. And redemption fits perfectly on the Sabbath. Tim Gombis thinks of a Christian Sabbath as an "alternative economy" (Gombis, *Mark*, 101).

Which claim explains the intensity of opposition in the final passage (3:1–6)? Again, what happens occurs on a Sabbath and in a synagogue. In fact, in the middle of a synagogue (3:3; NIV has "in front of everyone" but the expression is "in the middle" and probably means in the middle of the synagogue). The Pharisees, who are not mentioned until 3:6, "were looking for a reason to accuse Jesus" because they are agents of the temple who are hearing Jesus could be a disturber of the peace. Jesus chooses to play into their hands by challenging their Sabbath theology. He does it with a silencing question: "Which is lawful on the Sabbath: to do good or to do evil, to save life or to kill?" (3:4). No one wants to say "evil" but if they say "good" they may not be approved by the temple agents or their own Sabbath customs. Out of "anger" and grieving over their hard-heartedness, he heals the man's hand. Which, if we followed the plotline from 1:21 to this point, may well have led to crowds of people clapping and being amazed at Jesus. But Mark blunts the popularity theme with "the Pharisees" joining hands with those in line with Herod Antipas (the "Herodians") to "plot . . . how they might kill Jesus" (3:6).

All of this requests us to locate ourselves next to Jesus and alongside the disciples so we can feel the heat of reaction leading to rejection leading to plotting to kill Jesus. Mark foreshadows Jesus' crucifixion, and he implies that those who follow Jesus will be disciples of the Cross. Anyone who proposes liberation from existing customs will be opposed. The Pharisees did not oppose Jesus because they were evil or bad people. They are agents of a temple concerned with social disturbance, and Jesus' way of life will disturb traditionalists in Galilee.

QUESTIONS FOR REFLECTION AND APPLICATION

1. What do you learn about God from these five episodes?

2. How does Jesus feel and act toward people with disabilities?

3. Why do some of Jesus' critics oppose his healing of disabled people?

4. Why do you think some people are amazed by Jesus while others reject him?

5. How do Jesus' conflicts with the Pharisees compare with some of the conflicts about Jesus in our culture today?

FOR FURTHER READING

Louise A. Gosbel, "Disability and Paul," in *The Dictionary of Paul and His Letters*, ed. S. McKnight, Lynn H. Cohick, and Nijay K. Gupta (2nd ed.; Downers Grove, IL: IVP Academic, 2023), 228–231.

JESUS OF THE CROSS: AGENTS OF JESUS

Mark 3:7–19

7 Jesus withdrew with his disciples to the lake, and a large crowd from Galilee followed. 8 When they heard about all he was doing, many people came to him from Judea, Jerusalem, Idumea, and the regions across the Jordan and around Tyre and Sidon. 9 Because of the crowd he told his disciples to have a small boat ready for him, to keep the people from crowding him. 10 For he had healed many, so that those with diseases were pushing forward to touch him. 11 Whenever the impure spirits saw him, they fell down before him and cried out, "You are the Son of God." 12 But he gave them strict orders not to tell others about him.

13 Jesus went up on a mountainside and called to him those he wanted, and they came to him. 14 He appointed twelve that they might be with him and that he might send them out to preach 15 and to have authority to drive out demons. 16 These are the twelve he appointed: Simon (to whom he gave the name Peter), 17 James son of Zebedee and his brother John (to them he gave the name Boanerges, which means "sons of thunder"), 18 Andrew, Philip, Bartholomew, Matthew, Thomas, James son of Alphaeus, Thaddaeus, Simon the Zealot 19 and Judas Iscariot, who betrayed him.

The power of God at work through Jesus in Galilee led to a massive following. In Mark's first chapter the powers at work led to his growing popularity. That popularity provoked opposition and a plot to bring him down in chapter two, but in chapter three the popularity leads Jesus to distribute his ministry's gifts and powers to others. For many, popularity breeds a desire to make themselves more and more the center of the show. One cannot stop word of mouth spreading about one's powerful giftedness, but one can learn to use it for the good of others. Celebrity-ism can be avoided if one shares the platform and the glory. Which is what Jesus does in Mark chapter three.

POPULARITY GROWING

In the first paragraph of today's passage, the popularity of Jesus expands, seemingly out of control. In both Mark 3:7 and 3:8 Mark uses an expression that I translate as a "great mass" (NIV: "large crowd"), in 3:9 he uses "crowd," and in 3:10 we read of "many" who were "healed." Anyone who can heal people miraculously will attract both a crowd and all the terms used for crowds. In fact, fraudulent claims of healings will attract people, especially those most desperate for relief. One has to think the same occurred around Jesus.

The miraculous, Spirit-empowered cures in today's reading echo similar cures in the previous chapters. Jesus heals people from "diseases" (or "afflictions"; 3:10), and he liberates persons from "impure spirits," who, like the man in the synagogue, identify Jesus (cf. 3:11 with 1:24).

Notice something about Jesus. As I have said, those empowered by God with the gift of healing will attract crowds. I know a man named Tim who had the gift of

43

exorcism and most evenings when he got home from work a car or two was in his driveway. Inevitably, someone would plead for liberation from demons. He exercised his exorcisms with humility. Jesus, instead of being like the Rhinestone Cowboy who loved the lights and familiarity with Broadway (Glen Campbell), prohibited those who experienced liberation from the demons to talk about him (3:12). At least he tried. You can't silence the liberated. They have to talk (1:43, 45). What we notice about Jesus folds into two themes: he withdrew (1:38, 45; 3:7–9) and he pleaded with others not to reveal what he was doing (1:43; 3:12). Keeping his head down was his first strategy to deal with the rising opposition to his kingdom mission in Galilee. It's hard to keep your head down when your mission is tall enough to be seen by everyone, whether they are looking or not.

If we consider that Jesus is being inspected by temple agents because he is a potential disrupter of the peace, then one reason for silence is that he wanted things to be as quiet as possible. He could try, but those who experience miracles will not be silenced. So Jesus moves to a second strategy.

POWER DISTRIBUTED

Jesus' own strategy to gather the people of Galilee into his kingdom ran into conflict with his need to stay out of trouble. Jesus has launched the kingdom mission to liberate and redeem and save, all with a view to establishing God's rule, redemption, and will as God's empire over against all other empires in the world. He is now officially experiencing opposition to that mission and the opponents know Jesus is the Actor who matters most. So, he launches a second strategy when he decentralizes the actors by electing twelve. They are (1) "to be with him" so they can be sent (2) "to preach and (3) to have authority to drive out demons"

(3:14–15). Jesus here decentralizes the mission by distributing the powers to others. God's power is no zero-sum game. It is infinite and can be expanded and extended over and over. The Spirit's gifting is without limits, and it cares deeply about our bodies, especially those with disabilities in need of healing and social restoration.

These three elements are not the only elements of the mission of Jesus. The constant of these three is the necessity to spend time with Jesus—watching, listening, following, and associating with others who are doing the same. A much-loved pastor I know often asks his co-ministers, "What is Jesus saying to you today?" One would have to have a trusting relationship with someone to ask or answer that question. But if one has that, the question forms into the heart of discipleship and ministry. Whatever you are called to do begins with spending time with Jesus. Like reading the Gospel of Mark to be with Jesus.

Kingdom mission work, to which we are all summoned to participate, is always the Jesus-mission. It is never ours. We don't sit around and figure out what to do. We learn what Jesus did. Ours is *to extend and expand the mission of Jesus into our neighborhood and community.* Any redemptive work you find in Jesus or any leading of people to listen to and watch Jesus fit the kingdom mission. You don't have to be a pastor or a missionary. Whatever God calls you to do to participate in the holistic redemptive mission of Jesus is kingdom mission. Willa Cather, in her wonderful novel *Death Comes for the Archbishop,* said "you must follow the duty that calls loudest" (Cather, 208). What sounds loud to you may not be heard by others, but they are to hear their own loud calling.

The number twelve was not accidental. It was intentional, as intentional as John baptizing in the Jordan near the entry point for the children of Israel. As they were divided up into twelve tribes, so Jesus chooses twelve to be with him. Though some manuscripts have "whom he named apostles," the best manuscripts leave it at "twelve." We don't see the word "apostles" until Mark 6:30, but the verb *apostellō*, "sent," is found in today's passage (3:14). Regardless, the point remains true. Jesus selects twelve apostles to distribute kingdom power in order to expand the number of kingdom agents in Galilee. In so doing, they too will become indirect persons of concern to the temple-sent agents like the Pharisees and teachers of the law, with the backing at times of the Herodians.

From this moment on these twelve, and any persons associated with them, become disciples with a deeper embrace of the mission of Jesus. A mission now in conflict with the temple authorities. Which means the disciples, by going on this mission, embrace a cross-shaped life before they realize it will be a cross. *All disciples who participate in the mission of Jesus must embrace a cross-shaped life.* There is no other mission of Jesus to embrace. Participation in this mission is not for an elite group of the specially gifted. Jesus calls all of us into his mission. We offer him the gifts we are given.

But participation comes with a price. You, too, may find opposition when you embrace the kingdom mission in a Jesus-shaped life. God knows and Jesus is with you, because you are with him.

QUESTIONS FOR REFLECTION AND APPLICATION

1. What different strategies did Jesus use to navigate his growing fame and growing opposition?

2. How did Jesus begin to spread out his authority and mission to his disciples?

3. When Jesus called the twelve, do you think they understood the danger that put them in? Why or why not?

4. What duty or task from Jesus is calling loudly to you?

5. What is Jesus saying to you today?

FOR FURTHER READING

Glen Campbell, "Rhinestone Cowboy." Songwriters: Larry Weiss. Rhinestone Cowboy lyrics © Sony/ATV Music Publishing LLC, Warner Chappell Music, Inc.

Willa Cather, *Death Comes for the Archbishop* (Everyman's Library; New York: A.A. Knopf, 1992).

JESUS OF THE CROSS: TENSIONS IN A HOUSE

Mark 3:20–35

20 Then Jesus entered a house, and again a crowd gathered, so that he and his disciples were not even able to eat. 21 When his family heard about this, they went to take charge of him, for they said, "He is out of his mind."

> *22 And the teachers of the law who came down from Jerusalem said, "He is possessed by Beelzebul! By the prince of demons he is driving out demons."*
>
> *23 So Jesus called them over to him and began to speak to them in parables: "How can Satan drive out Satan? 24 If a kingdom is divided against itself, that kingdom cannot stand. 25 If a house is divided against itself, that house cannot stand. 26 And if Satan opposes himself and is divided, he cannot stand; his end has come. 27 In fact, no one can enter a strong man's house without first tying him up. Then he can plunder the strong man's house. 28 Truly I tell you, people can be forgiven all their sins and every slander they utter, 29 but whoever blasphemes against the Holy Spirit will never be forgiven; they are guilty of an eternal sin."*

30 He said this because they were saying, "He has an impure spirit."

31 Then Jesus' mother and brothers arrived. Standing outside, they sent someone in to call him. 32 A crowd was sitting around him, and they told him, "Your mother and brothers are outside looking for you."

33 "Who are my mother and my brothers?" he asked.

34 Then he looked at those seated in a circle around him and said, "Here are my mother and my brothers! 35 Whoever does God's will is my brother and sister and mother."

Have you ever noticed how often Jesus is at a table or in a home, or house? The weight of today's passage occurs in a house (3:20, 31), probably the same house. The house for the section about Jesus' family (3:20, 31–35) probably happens at Peter's house. (At least I think that's the best suggestion.) Either way, Jesus' tension with others does not always occur in a synagogue or in some public place. Today's passage records tensions smack-dab in the middle of someone's home.

The three sections (reformatted above) are organized in what is sometimes called a "sandwich" structure. Like a sandwich with bread, filling, bread. At the top of this sandwich-passage is family (3:20–21), then we read about teachers of the law (3:22–30), and then we return to family (3:31–35). That kind of organization is not accidental. The substance in the middle helps us understand the bread around it. Or, if you prefer, the bread clarifies what's between the pieces of bread. Here's how it works: the concern of Jesus' family over the conflict he has created finds expression in the "teachers of the law" thinking Jesus is in league with the evil one. Which is what his family then expresses in 3:21 when they mutter that Jesus is "out of his mind," language that elsewhere in Mark is used only for those under the influence of demons! So, they hightail it down from Nazareth to Capernaum to find Jesus in that house Jesus entered (3:20). There they summon Jesus, and Jesus will have none of it. He once again calls people to a radical, even opposed, discipleship (3:31–35).

OPPOSITION

Conflict often descends rapidly into name-calling and in some cases to the ultimate label: demonic. The conflict in Galilee over the attraction of the populace to Jesus descends precisely to that label. The labelers are the experts in the law, and so influential is their label for Jesus his own family has more or less endorsed it (3:21).

The redemptive act of Jesus we call exorcism draws the allegation that Jesus is casting out demons by the power of "Beelzebul," and a simple translation of this term is "prince of demons" (3:22). In other words, his opponents contend Jesus' powerful works are deceptive frauds because they are achieved by an "impure spirit" (3:30). Labels often work. Some today who pursue justice are called socialists, while such persons think they are following Jesus in the way of justice and peace. Victims of power abuse who blow the whistle are sometimes labeled as divisive or even demonic. Calling truth demonic is close to what Jesus in this very passage calls unforgivable.

Jesus deconstructs their allegation with a question that turns their allegation inside-out or upside-down: "How can Satan drive out Satan?" That would lead to a divided kingdom or house (3:23–26). He then turns that into his penchant form of teaching, that is, a riddle-like story: *The only one who can plunder a strong man's house [Satan] without overpowering the strong man* (3:27). All to say that if he has the power to exorcise demons then he must be more powerful than the demons.

His commentary on that personal claim is that the experts in the law better realize they are making serious claims that reach into the presence of God. His power to exorcise is from the Spirit, and denunciation of the Spirit's work in this world is unforgivable because it is an "eternal sin" (3:29). They can say what they want about Jesus, but they dare not accuse redemptive work with evil work. To call something good evil blasphemes the God of the good. To dig in one's heels against the good work Jesus is doing is to set oneself on a path that leads to destruction. The sin that is unforgivable is not a momentary act of recklessness, but a posture taken toward the work of God in this world. It is not forgivable because the person refuses to repent and acknowledge the truth of God.

FAMILY

Mark's sandwiching of Jesus' family with the teachers of the law leads us to see their seeming endorsement of the labels his opponents are pinning on Jesus in 3:21 as well as their attempt to rescue Jesus from danger and, to put it bluntly, from himself. They think his mission is off the rails because the leaders of the people in Galilee, the scribes and Pharisees, find Jesus' mission off the rails. So they decide to go down from Nazareth to Capernaum to have a word with Jesus. We should locate ourselves with them for the moment. Their concerns are familial—their son and brother is in deep trouble with the wrong people. Their concerns are social—Jesus is offending enough people that word from Capernaum has gotten all the way to his home village, Nazareth. Their concerns are traditional—who better to trust than the religious leaders of your community? (The scribes in this case.) Their concerns are political—word is out that Jesus could be drawing the attention of Herod Antipas, Rome's agent of "peace" (called *pax Romana*). Their concerns are safety—opposition to Jesus includes them, and they don't want any part in it. Aren't all our "spiritual" concerns wrapped up in other concerns?

So they march down to Peter's home, summon Jesus away from his small circle of followers and out for a conversation. He turns them away with strong words: "Who are my mother and my brothers?" (3:33). His strategy of forming a kingdom coalition includes forming all as kingdom-mission siblings, and the heart of that siblingship is the twelve. His true siblings now are his disciples. With the implicit invitation for his own family to cross the threshold of Peter's home and to sit in the circle around him. The kingdom coalition points only at those who do "God's will" (3:35).

All in a house. Peter's house. Not out in the open but in the privacy and safety of a home that is the mission station for Jesus' kingdom mission in Galilee. The conflict at work with temple agents and Herodians comes up in Peter's home. No one is safe from the labels and potential death for associating with Jesus. The temple agents know Rome is watching. Jesus calls his followers to gather, to listen, to learn, and to follow him to Jerusalem and into the hands of his Father. That's what it means to follow Jesus, as we learned when we took a deep dive into Mark 8:27–9:1.

QUESTIONS FOR REFLECTION AND APPLICATION

1. What is the substance of the sin Jesus calls "blaspheming the Holy Spirit"?

2. What drives the concerns Jesus' family has about him?

3. How does Jesus reorient family relationships with his kingdom mission?

4. How have you seen truth labeled dangerous or even demonic in church cultures?

5. Can you think of a time you have expressed a "spiritual" concern for someone, like Jesus' family does for him, that was actually wrapped up in other concerns?

JESUS OF THE CROSS: THE STORYTELLER

Mark 4:1–20

¹ Again Jesus began to teach by the lake. The crowd that gathered around him was so large that he got into a boat and sat in it out on the lake, while all the people were along the shore at the water's edge. ² He taught them many things by parables, and in his teaching said: ³ "Listen! A farmer went out to sow his seed. ⁴ As he was scattering the seed, some fell along the path, and the birds came and ate it up. ⁵ Some fell on rocky places, where it did not have much soil. It sprang up quickly, because the soil was shallow. ⁶ But when the sun came up, the plants were scorched, and they withered because they had no root. ⁷ Other seed fell among thorns, which grew up and choked the plants, so that they did not bear grain. ⁸ Still other seed fell on good soil. It came up, grew and produced a crop, some multiplying thirty, some sixty, some a hundred times."

⁹ Then Jesus said, "Whoever has ears to hear, let them hear."

¹⁰ When he was alone, the Twelve and the others around him asked him about the parables. ¹¹ He told them, "The secret of the kingdom of God has been given to you. But to those on the outside everything is said in parables ¹² so that,

they may be ever seeing but never perceiving,
and ever hearing but never understanding;
otherwise they might turn and be forgiven!'"

 [13] Then Jesus said to them, "Don't you understand this parable? How then will you understand any parable? [14] The farmer sows the word. [15] Some people are like seed along the path, where the word is sown. As soon as they hear it, Satan comes and takes away the word that was sown in them. [16] Others, like seed sown on rocky places, hear the word and at once receive it with joy. [17] But since they have no root, they last only a short time. When trouble or persecution comes because of the word, they quickly fall away. [18] Still others, like seed sown among thorns, hear the word; [19] but the worries of this life, the deceitfulness of wealth and the desires for other things come in and choke the word, making it unfruitful. [20] Others, like seed sown on good soil, hear the word, accept it, and produce a crop—some thirty, some sixty, some a hundred times what was sown."

Not only did Jesus tell people not to talk about him, and not only did he withdraw from the crowds, but he told stories shorter than short stories that subverted the stories of those representing Rome and the temple authorities. These stories are called "parables," and a parable is something laid down next to something else that helps to explain what is next to it. So he told these parables to help his audiences understand the kingdom of God. Yet, his stories were cryptic enough that many did not understand what he was getting at. Even more, part of Jesus' subversive strategy of going underground as much as possible was so his opponents would not understand what he was teaching his followers. His strategy of going underground, let's face the facts, did not work very well. The crowds were not about to be silenced.

A Parable Explained

Jesus tells a short story about a farmer who tossed out seeds onto four different soils: a hard path, on rocky places, among thorns, on fertile soil (4:3–8). Only the good soil yielded a good harvest. Jesus then explains this story to the disciples who did not comprehend what he was saying (4:10, 13). In an allegorical style, the farmer sows the "word." The hard path describes Satan snatching the seeds; the rocky soil points to those who respond to the kingdom mission immediately but don't stick around when opposition knocks on the door; the thorns reveal that some seeds get choked out by the world's worries and wealth; while the good soil paints a picture of those who respond in faith and allegiance to Jesus and so flourish in the life God wants (4:14–20).

Parables Defined

What's a Parable?

Jesus was not alone in telling parables as they were favorites of Jewish teachers. Parables are imaginative analogies, that is uber short-stories, designed to offer an alternative worldview. That is, Jesus tells a little story with a character or two or three and the attentive listener enters through the imagination to envision that short story occurring. In entering into that story Jesus often surprises the reader with some little detail that is designed to shift that person's worldview. Jesus' parables invite us to "imagine a world like this," and the world he wants us to imagine is the kingdom of God.

How to Interpret a Parable

To interpret a parable of Jesus we need to read the story carefully in a quest to *determine the central analogy Jesus is making*. The short story is "laid next to" (that's a literal translation of "parable" in Greek) something about a kingdom worldview, so the quest is to figure out what connects them. That is, what is the comparison? It is important as well to stick to the 1st Century Jewish world of Jesus to make sense of the parable. We should not think in this passage of farming in Iowa and Nebraska. As well, we can keep our eyes on the individual Gospel's themes and bigger context for helping us see what Jesus teaches here. And, remember that reading a parable is more than exercise in detecting a purpose. These parables are meant to transform the hearers and, now that they are written out, the readers (like you and me).

One warning: avoid getting cute and finding hidden treasures that distract us from the central analogy. The rocky soil is not something specific, like the Sadducees. We can imagine seed falling on rocky soil where seeds can't take root. That gives us plenty of space for our imaginations to kick in to experience such a reality in our world.

New Testament Everyday Bible Study:
Luke *(McKnight), pp. 123–125*

A PARABLE STRATEGY

The disciples, though they have listened carefully, don't quite get the point of the parable when Jesus first tells it. So they ask and, in asking, will hear a response from Jesus that clarifies his strategy for parables. He tells them for his disciples to whom "the secret of the kingdom of God has been given" (4:11). Puffy chests were visible on the disciples to know how privileged they were, even if some of their minds were still baffled. A proud person with confusion is not ready for the conflict that is mounting in Galilee and Jerusalem. One has to wonder if the puffiness was not poked by Jesus with a pin. The "secret" of the kingdom, as Tim Gombis concludes, "has to do with its cross-shaped character. Jesus is a cross-oriented Messiah who defies the expectations of his culture. He is not impressive by human standards. He is not a military hero who will play to the national longings for vengeance against the Romans. He will not confer social capital and prestige on those who follow him" (Gombis, *Mark*, 141).

More significantly, Jesus ties his strategy for going underground with parables to the prophet Isaiah, who made it clear that, because some were so hard-hearted and resistant to the message of the prophet, some teachings were given that blinded the minds of those who heard them (4:10–12). Morna Hooker's summary statement expresses the purpose of parables well: "the parables both reveal and conceal: for those who have ears to hear they convey the good news of the Kingdom, to those who refuse to listen their message is obscure" (Hooker, *Mark*, 120).

You would not be alone to think this seems harsh, almost like God had a list of the unworthy away from whom God had turned. But such a view not only crashes into the God of love in the Bible, but it fails to hear these words in the context of the mission of Jesus that is opposed by the strategies of the temple state to maintain control. Jesus is on a mission to disrupt their power. To do that, he tells stories that outsiders will not comprehend *so he can deepen discipleship for the disciples and stall the opposition as he mentors his followers.*

Those who respond affirmatively to Jesus are like those in the house who are encircling Jesus to listen to him and who are doing God's will (3:31–35).

A Parable's Truth

The truth of this parable is crystal clear: kingdom mission will often involve opposition to kingdom mission. Or, to put it differently, not everyone's gonna jump on board. Not that we can calculate three out of four will not become faithful followers. These soils represent Jesus' earliest sketch of how people are responding to the mission. Mark's Gospel so far makes it look like *everyone loves Jesus* except those sent by the temple authorities to clue in the crowds that Jesus is off the rails and might get us all in trouble. That "everyone loves Jesus" of Mark exaggerates the reality, and we know this because in this parable Jesus paints various forms of final rejection of the mission. Mark, like most preachers, exaggerates.

If kingdom mission means liberation from evil, forgiveness of sinners otherwise deemed marginal, and a summons to turn one's life over to Jesus, then kingdom mission will not be popular. Those in power and benefiting from evil will often fight against liberation; those who think the marginal, the weak, the disabled, women, and minorities should be ignored will resist forgiveness and restoration. Have a conversation with peace advocates, with those fighting for symbolic memory of what we did to Native Americans, or with those who know our farming methods are destroying the world's topsoils. Or, as I have done for three years, seek to get those in power to form policies and procedures that protect and even favor those abused and victimized by church authorities. Worse yet, more people will not care—the thorns imagery—because they'd rather be caught up in their worries and wealth.

The conflict in Galilee between the temple authorities and Jesus' kingdom mission are fueled by cosmic theft (Satan; 4:15), discipleship shallowness (4:17), physical and bodily threats (4:17), and satisfaction with the pleasures of life (4:19). As it was then, so it is now. The kingdom mission invades life with a challenge to take up the cross and follow the Jesus of the Cross who is just ahead of us on the path to the kingdom of God.

Perhaps you ask, what makes for a flourishing and fruitful fertile soil? It means being with Jesus and that means trusting him, listening to him, adoring and worshiping him, watching him, and learning to walk—as a child learns to pedal and balance a bicycle—on the cross-path when we can't see Jesus.

QUESTIONS FOR REFLECTION AND APPLICATION

1. Why does Jesus speak in parables?

2. What is the purpose of these short stories?

3. How does Jesus say different people will respond to him?

4. In which "soil" do you see yourself?

5. What is your favorite parable from Jesus, either from Mark or another Gospel?

JESUS OF THE CROSS: REVEALING AND REMINDING

Mark 4:21–25

²¹ He said to them, "Do you bring in a lamp to put it under a bowl or a bed? Instead, don't you put it on its stand? ²² For whatever is hidden is meant to be disclosed, and whatever is concealed is meant to be brought out into the open. ²³ If anyone has ears to hear, let them hear."

²⁴ "Consider carefully what you hear," he continued. "With the measure you use, it will be measured to you—and even more. ²⁵ Whoever has will be given more; whoever does not have, even what they have will be taken from them."

At times in reading the Gospel of Mark one runs into seemingly random moments where Mark could have said, *Where do I put these sayings by our Lord? Here's where they fit, even if it's a bit of an interruption.* Mark 4:21–25 strikes me that way. The verses fit here because Jesus has just disclosed that parables are meant for his followers and not for the public, especially not for the temple agents at work in

Galilee. The two sayings of today's passage help all of Mark's readers comprehend Jesus' strategy in telling parables.

First, his strategy for parables is to *reveal* because they take what is hidden and bring it "out into the open," even if they need some explanation (4:13–20). As one places a lamp so its light can dispel darkness, and as God wants to make known the hidden and concealed truths (the secret of the kingdom in 4:11), so Jesus tells his followers his special parables (4:21–23). Jesus knows his parables will be an ambiguous message to the outsider. But, for the insider they become a revelation both that the kingdom has been launched and that they are given the opportunity to enter into the kingdom story.

Second, his strategy for parables is to *remind* his disciples, those who comprehend them, that they are accountable to God to live according to the vision of those parables. They are to listen to his revelations and to see (the word "consider" translates the common word for "see" [*blepō*]), or imagine, the world that he sketches in his parables. A kind of *Do you see what the kingdom is like?* His next two sentences are about accountability before God: the "measure" used by them will be used by God on them, and positive receptions of Jesus' revelations will lead to an abundant harvest just as impartial responses to Jesus will not last (cf. 4:20 with 4:25a; 4:16–19 with 4:25b).

Keep both of these in mind as we turn to the next passage, which contains two of Jesus' parables.

QUESTIONS FOR REFLECTION AND APPLICATION

1. What are Jesus' two strategies for parables?

2. How do his analogies here help explain his strategies?

3. What kind of vision does Jesus convey with his short stories?

4. How do Jesus' parables spark your imagination?

5. Have you ever struggled to understand Jesus' teaching in parables? What was that experience like for you?

JESUS OF THE CROSS: KINGDOM IMAGINATION

Mark 4:26–34

26 He also said, "This is what the kingdom of God is like. A man scatters seed on the ground. 27 Night and day, whether he sleeps or gets up, the seed sprouts and grows, though he does not know how. 28 All by itself the soil produces grain—first the stalk, then the head, then the full kernel in the head. 29 As soon as the grain is ripe, he puts the sickle to it, because the harvest has come."

30 Again he said, "What shall we say the kingdom of God is like, or what parable shall we use to describe it? 31 It is like a mustard seed, which is the smallest of all seeds on earth. 32 Yet when planted, it grows and becomes the largest of all garden plants, with such big branches that the birds can perch in its shade."

33 With many similar parables Jesus spoke the word to them, as much as they could understand. 34 He did not say anything to them without using a parable. But when he was alone with his own disciples, he explained everything.

Imagine a world Jesus reveals to his disciples in these parables where God's holistic redemption works underground but quietly and, surprisingly effectively, produces grain and seed. Quietly, surprisingly—two potent words for anyone who wants to come to terms with what Jesus means by kingdom. His words crash into our plans and schemes on a daily basis. These two parables reveal the nature of the kingdom, but other passages will remind the disciples of their need to respond.

PEOPLE LIKE A SHOW

If you say "kingdom" people think of castles and kings and territories and armies and battles and festivals. Not for Jesus. Just as Jesus combined Messiah with cross and discipleship with self-denial, so he hitched kingdom to a secret, sacred mystery. As an expert on parables once wrote, "Claims about the presence of the kingdom are no more compelling now than earlier, probably less so" (Snodgrass, *Stories with Intent*, 190). He launched the kingdom, but it was an "all by itself" underground activity of God's redemptive work.

The show impresses people, attracts people, and wows people. But shows fade into obscurity. Attaching Jesus to the show fails the fundamentals of his kingdom imagination. The kingdom, instead, was a slow, secretive work that over time produced grain (4:26–29). Computer technology forms us into humans who know, expect, and then desire and need immediacy. Kingdom crashes into immediacy with the message of slow work and slow redemption and slow transformation. We are called to trust the faithful work of God and to wait for its appearing. It will because the kingdom has been launched, it's at work, and it will produce the harvest God has designed.

At the bottom of this simplest of all parables is that the man was asleep. As the great Methodist scholar, quoting what another once said, it shows that kingdom is "God's seed not humanity's deed" (C.K. Barrett, *Preaching*, 73). And God's seed is a hidden power at work underground. The man was asleep, and it grew in ways he did not understand but most importantly it grew without his help or manipulation. Parables never teach the whole truth. A man asleep does not mean we don't have to do anything. Other parables will turn to the need for human response, but the truth of this parable remains: God's seed does God's work.

PEOPLE LIKE BIG

As people like a show, they devalue the small, the minuscule. People like what is big and noisy and extravagant. The kingdom is not a chestnut-sized nut but a mustard seed. Tiny. But when the mustard seed germinates in fertile soil with adequate moisture the seed becomes "the largest of all garden plants" (4:32). Jesus trades in boilerplate images: smallest of all seeds, which a botanist told me is not true, and the biggest plant in the garden, about which one has to ask, *Whose garden?* Getting lost in such a technicality misses the point: what some perceive as insignificant can become significant in the plan of God. This parable does not emphasize growth as much as it does the extreme contrast of small beginnings with big endings.

Jesus was dismissed as a Galilean, as the son of a mother whom some thought had been unfaithful, as an untrained teacher, and as one crucified as a criminal. His disciples came from the margins of society. Jesus wrote the script for how not to create a universal movement. How could such a person be the Messiah and how could his work be called God's kingdom? The only reason we say such things is because we are like everyone else: we like the show, we like the big.

God does what God does, and what God does is called kingdom. And kingdom means a quiet, irresistible revolution that liberates and redeems and transforms. Look by the show and the big and watch God work in the hidden corners of your community.

Questions for Reflection and Application

1. How does the slowness of God's kingdom conflict with our addiction to immediacy?

2. What does the first parable teach about seed?

3. What does the second parable teach about seed?

4. What markers of Jesus' identity did people use to dismiss him?

5. How are God's seeds at work in your life?

FOR FURTHER READING

C.K. Barrett, *Preaching Methodist Theology and Biblical Truth: Classic Sermons of C.K. Barrett* (ed. Ben Witherington III; Nashville: Wesley's Foundery Book, 2017).

Klyne Snodgrass, *Stories with Intent: A Comprehensive Guide to the Parables of Jesus* (2nd edition; Grand Rapids: Eerdmans, 2018).

JESUS OF THE CROSS: POWER OVER THE SEA

Mark 4:35–41

35 *That day when evening came, he said to his disciples, "Let us go over to the other side."* 36 *Leaving the crowd behind, they took him along, just as he was, in the boat. There were also other boats with him.* 37 *A furious squall came up, and the waves broke over the boat, so that it was nearly swamped.* 38 *Jesus was in the stern, sleeping on a cushion. The disciples woke him and said to him, "Teacher, don't you care if we drown?"*

39 *He got up, rebuked the wind and said to the waves, "Quiet! Be still!" Then the wind died down and it was completely calm.*

40 *He said to his disciples, "Why are you so afraid? Do you still have no faith?"*

41 *They were terrified and asked each other, "Who is this? Even the wind and the waves obey him!"*

The pressure the crowds were putting on Jesus' reputation and the tension his fame was putting on the temple agents, who were worried about uprisings, leads often in the Gospels to Jesus' need to seek solitude and privacy. In today's passage Jesus and his disciples cross the Sea of Galilee from the northern area to a region south and east. Mark 4:35 says "to the other side," which means to the eastern shore. But 5:1 then says, "they went across the lake to the region of the Gerasenes," which also means the eastern shore. Matthew clarifies that the "furious squall" happened on the trip to the other side (Matthew 8:23–26).

QUESTION ONE: WHAT KIND OF MIRACLE IS THIS?

We call knocking the wind out of a "furious squall" a "nature" miracle because the act of God is upon the natural world rather than upon a human. Begin with this: If Jesus is either God incarnate or in touch with God in a unique way, and I believe both are true, the question is not *Can such things happen?* but *Can God do such things?* The answers are both Yes. Yet, the nature miracles stand out even from the exorcism to follow in Mark 5 or the healing miracles and the stunning reality of the resurrection of Jesus. For myself, if God raised Jesus from the dead, then nature miracles become all the more credible.

Nature Miracles

1. The large catch of fish (Luke 5:1–11; John 21:4–14)
2. Coin in a fish's mouth (Matthew 17:24–27)
3. Stilling a storm (Mark 4:35–41)
4. Feeding multitudes (Mark 6:32–44; 8:1–10)
5. Walking on the sea (Mark 6:45–52)
6. Withering a fig tree (Mark 11:12–14, 20–26)
7. Turning water into wine (John 2:1–12)

QUESTION TWO: WHO IS HE?

The passage does not close down. Instead, it opens up a world of wondering: "Who is this? Even the wind and the waves obey him" (4:41). When this passage is read well it leads us not to history, as in *Could this have happened?*, but to Christology, as in, *If Jesus did this, who could he be?* Many readers of Mark take us wisely straight to the Old Testament, to passages like Exodus 14:21–31 or to Psalm 29:3–10 or 89:8–9 and 107:23–32 or to Jonah 1:1–16. Each of these passages reveals a God who controls the waters. The *Who is he?* question then leads to the *Is he God?* question. As the great preacher Gardner Taylor said in a sermon, "Jesus got up from his sleep, weary like I am, but able to do what I cannot do, what no half god can do, and what no counterfeit god can do. He got up, rubbed the cobwebs out of his eyes, and leaned over to the roaring sea. . . . The wind heard the Savior's voice and ran back to its hiding place in the hills. . . . The waves stretched humbly at his feet" (Taylor, *The Words of Gardner Taylor*, 97–98). Now you tell me, who is he?

Today's passage starts to end on a downer: the disciples asked that question because "they were terrified" (NIV) or "they were scared with a great scare" (Mark 4:41). Their scare and panic stands opposed to Jesus' calm and sleep (4:38, 41). His pointed-finger questioning of them might make us wonder if he did not expect them to calm the storm. After all, he had distributed his power and authority to them (3:15). Their question *Who is he?* is followed by another: "Even the winds and waves obey him!" (4:41). That's the beginning of a good answer.

QUESTION THREE: WHAT ABOUT US?

The natural question you and I may ask is *Does God still do this kind of thing?* Most of us would answer *Not in my life so far.*

But in reading Craig Keener's amazing books about miracles, one can close down his extensive collection of detailed stories into the conclusion that *Well, yes, God still does.* Most of us, too, respond as the disciples do when we encounter a squall in life: "Teacher, don't you care if we drown?" (4:38). That is, we are tempted to blame God for not fixing our squalls. Jesus has a right to chide those close followers for being "afraid," which is not criticism of their emotions but instead a challenge for them to trust the one they've already witnessed doing so many great things. Notice these acts of power: 1:21–28, 29–34, 40–45; 2:1–12; 3:1–6. Remembering what God has done inspires a person to trust God in life's squalls. To bolster our confidence in Jesus, and to help us answer the *Who is he?* question, we can turn to the next three passages, each of which records another mighty miracle by Jesus: an exorcism (5:1–20) and a double-story in healing a sick woman and raising a dead girl (5:21–43).

QUESTIONS FOR REFLECTION AND APPLICATION

1. Which miracles give you more awe, Jesus' healing miracles or his nature miracles?

2. What do you think this nature miracle says about who Jesus is?

3. Have you witnessed any miracles in your life?

4. Have you ever had a moment of wondering something similar to, "Teacher, don't you care if we drown?" How did God respond to your prayer?

5. How does Jesus' challenge to the disciples about fear and faith impact your life of discipleship?

FOR FURTHER READING

Gardner C. Taylor, *The Words of Gardner Taylor.*
   Volume 3: Quintessential Classics: 1980– Present
   (compiled by Edward L. Taylor; Valley Forge:
   Judson Press, 2000).
Craig S. Keener, *Miracles. 2 Volumes* (Grand Rapids:
   Baker Academic, 2011).

JESUS OF THE CROSS: POWER OVER THE DEMONS

Mark 5:1–20

¹ They went across the lake to the region of the Gerasenes. ² When Jesus got out of the boat, a man with an impure spirit came from the tombs to meet him. ³ This man lived in the tombs, and no one could bind him anymore, not even with a chain. ⁴ For he had often been chained hand and foot, but he tore the chains apart and broke the irons on his feet. No one was strong enough to subdue him. ⁵ Night and day among the tombs and in the hills he would cry out and cut himself with stones.

⁶ When he saw Jesus from a distance, he ran and fell on his knees in front of him. ⁷ He shouted at the top of his voice, "What do you want with me, Jesus, Son of the Most High God? In God's name don't torture me!" ⁸ For Jesus had said to him, "Come out of this man, you impure spirit!"

⁹ Then Jesus asked him, "What is your name?"

"My name is Legion," he replied, "for we are many."

¹⁰ And he begged Jesus again and again not to send them out of the area.

[11] *A large herd of pigs was feeding on the nearby hillside.*
[12] *The demons begged Jesus, "Send us among the pigs; allow us to go into them."* *[13]* *He gave them permission, and the impure spirits came out and went into the pigs. The herd, about two thousand in number, rushed down the steep bank into the lake and were drowned.*

[14] *Those tending the pigs ran off and reported this in the town and countryside, and the people went out to see what had happened.* *[15]* *When they came to Jesus, they saw the man who had been possessed by the legion of demons, sitting there, dressed and in his right mind; and they were afraid.* *[16]* *Those who had seen it told the people what had happened to the demon-possessed man—and told about the pigs as well.* *[17]* *Then the people began to plead with Jesus to leave their region.*

[18] *As Jesus was getting into the boat, the man who had been demon-possessed begged to go with him.* *[19]* *Jesus did not let him, but said, "Go home to your own people and tell them how much the Lord has done for you, and how he has had mercy on you."* *[20]* *So the man went away and began to tell in the Decapolis how much Jesus had done for him. And all the people were amazed.*

Today's passage portrays in graphic images a tragic condition for someone created in God's image. Before anyone gets to diagnosing this man's condition, we need to vault over all the details to almost the end of the passage. Down in verse fifteen we discover Jesus did something to this man that led people to say he "was sitting there, dressed and in his right mind" (5:15) and then we read that the liberated man "began to tell in the Decapolis how much Jesus had done for him" (5:20). However we diagnose this man's condition, he was out of sorts with God, with himself, and with his community. So Jesus demolished his alienations and re-located him squarely into his community as a witness to God, to Jesus, and to the gospel of the kingdom. The solution, community, reveals the problem, comprehensive alienation.

ALIENATED

The man's problem was that he was captured by an abundance of "impure spirits" or "demons" (5:2, 13, 15). The modern world believes everything can be explained by science at the material level, and if it can't be, it will be. The world of Jesus was not materialistic but, alongside the material there was another world, one inhabited by and haunted by cosmic, invisible powers, all under the rule of Satan, the Devil or the Evil One. The same cosmic reality describes our world too, even if some deny it or explain it away. The one thing the prince of demons wants is alienation from God, from the self, and from others. It had this man in its grip, so much so he says his name is "Legion," which was the common military term for something like 5,000+ soldiers.

Mark's depiction in the first paragraph, brief though it may be, sketches a man utterly alienated from God, from himself, and from others. For a Jewish writer, living in the "region of the Gerasenes" (the location is disputed) locates the man among the pagan gentiles. Alienation from God shows up in the "impure spirit" as well as dwelling in a cemetery. The evil one's aim is death, and this man lives among the dead. His demonic capture somehow provides uber-human powers, and his voice of bellowing and his embodied acts of cutting demonstrate a man in the deepest of pains. Psychological diagnoses don't explain the man. The demons captured him.

LIBERATED

Jesus liberated the captured man. One of the more remarkable features of the Gospels stories about evil, invisible cosmic powers are that those captured often immediately recognize Jesus for who he is (1:24; 3:11). The spirits know the One of the Spirit. As the Father identified Jesus as the Son, so the spirits (cf. 1:11; 5:7). Instead of having a conversation with them, Jesus looks through them and demands their departure.

What happens next dances back and forth from the unusual, if not bizarre, to the obvious. Jesus yanks the spirits out of the man and, at their request because somewhere is better than the emptiness of nowhere, implants them in a herd, some 2,000—that's one big herd—of pigs, which indicate not only a gentile territory but also something unclean. They run pell-mell down a hill into the sea and drown. Yes, both unusual (another nature miracle of sorts) and obvious: gentile, pagan, unclean, demons. A man is liberated from all that alienated him from God, from self, and from others.

The pig farmers, observing the bizarre event, hightail it back to the community, the community comes out to the shore to confirm the story, they confirm the story, and then go into community-protection. Instead of being like the crowds of Galilee, who were amazed at Jesus, this community pleads with Jesus "to leave their region" (5:17). The oddity of it all is that they saw the cemetery man "sitting there, dressed and in his right mind" and this caused fear in them (5:15). Instead of gratitude for the work of Jesus to restore someone to their community, instead of receiving the elimination of the man of pain, they won't face a fresh form of liberation. Encounter with God, with the powers of God, with the Lord over the spirits, instead of prompting worship and amazement, prompts the kind of fear that wants to be shielded from Jesus and his kingdom mission. Humans at times aren't willing to face truth and transparency.

Restored

For me the decisive moment of this passage was just quoted above: "sitting there, dressed and in his right mind" (5:15). There's a calmness about him, like finding some child after eating too much candy and running through the house in a frenzy with all sorts of hops and skips, suddenly sitting down for a cup of tea and a conversation with mom and dad. Back in clothing shows yet another element of this story: his pain had driven him to nakedness or near-nakedness. Sitting and robed, and thus in a common civil appearance, Mark tells us he was now restored to "his right mind." He's sensible. His wits are about him. Surely he felt like he was waking from a horrific nightmare. No one knows liberation more than the liberated.

Commissioned

The now-sensible man desires to become what the disciples of Jesus are: companions of Jesus. He "begged" Jesus to "go with him" (5:18) but Jesus knew the man had been appointed by God to be what Paul would become: a man called to declare the good news to the gentiles. So, Jesus says "Go home to your own people and tell them how much the Lord has done for you, and how he has had mercy on you" (5:19). Unlike Jonah, this man goes, and Mark, not so subtly, switches from "Lord" to "Jesus" (5:20) to make it clear that Jesus is the Lord even over the demons. The liberated man's evangelistic endeavors circulated in the "Decapolis," which is a ten-city league of Hellenistic (gentile) cities. Each was in league with Rome, and each was independent, one of which was Scythopolis (Old Testament's Beth Shean), which is on many tours of the Holy Land today. It is good news to readers that after his preaching "all the people were amazed" (5:20).

QUESTIONS FOR REFLECTION AND APPLICATION

1. What role does community alienation play in many of Jesus' healing miracles?

2. Why do you think that not all of the people Jesus healed became his followers?

3. What do you make of the near total absence of the disciples in this story? "They" in 5:1 indicates they're present but then they disappear.

4. What in your life needs Jesus' liberating and restoring work?

5. How would your church respond to a person with these symptoms?

JESUS OF THE CROSS: POWER OVER DEATH AND DISEASE

Mark 5:21–43

²¹ *When Jesus had again crossed over by boat to the other side of the lake, a large crowd gathered around him while he was by the lake.* ²² *Then one of the synagogue leaders, named Jairus, came, and when he saw Jesus, he fell at his feet.* ²³ *He pleaded earnestly with him, "My little daughter is dying. Please come and put your hands on her so that she will be healed and live."* ²⁴ *So Jesus went with him.*

A large crowd followed and pressed around him.

²⁵ *And a woman was there who had been subject to bleeding for twelve years.* ²⁶ *She had suffered a great deal under the care of many doctors and had spent all she had, yet instead of getting better she grew worse.* ²⁷ *When she heard about Jesus, she came up behind him in the crowd and touched his cloak,* ²⁸ *because she thought, "If I just touch his clothes, I will be healed."* ²⁹ *Immediately her bleeding stopped and she felt in her body that she was freed from her suffering.* ³⁰ *At once Jesus*

realized that power had gone out from him. He turned around in the crowd and asked, "Who touched my clothes?"

³¹ "You see the people crowding against you," his disciples answered, "and yet you can ask, 'Who touched me?' "

³² But Jesus kept looking around to see who had done it. ³³ Then the woman, knowing what had happened to her, came and fell at his feet and, trembling with fear, told him the whole truth. ³⁴ He said to her, "Daughter, your faith has healed you. Go in peace and be freed from your suffering."

³⁵ While Jesus was still speaking, some people came from the house of Jairus, the synagogue leader. "Your daughter is dead," they said. "Why bother the teacher anymore?"

³⁶ Overhearing what they said, Jesus told him, "Don't be afraid; just believe."

³⁷ He did not let anyone follow him except Peter, James and John the brother of James. ³⁸ When they came to the home of the synagogue leader, Jesus saw a commotion, with people crying and wailing loudly. ³⁹ He went in and said to them, "Why all this commotion and wailing? The child is not dead but asleep." ⁴⁰ But they laughed at him.

After he put them all out, he took the child's father and mother and the disciples who were with him, and went in where the child was.

⁴¹ He took her by the hand and said to her, "Talitha koum!" (which means "Little girl, I say to you, get up!"). ⁴² Immediately the girl stood up and began to walk around (she was twelve years old). At this they were completely astonished. ⁴³ He gave strict orders not to let anyone know about this, and told them to give her something to eat.

Like a previous passage (3:20–35), today's passage is another example of Mark's sandwich structure. It begins with a story about Jairus' twelve-year-old daughter dying, it moves into a story about a woman whose menstruation makes her perpetually unclean, among other experiences that reveal the woman to be what we would call disabled, and then returns to Jairus' daughter who had just died. I reformatted the passage above to make the structure more visible. The previous stories, the stories of today's reading, and the stories of Jesus' compassionate miracles and healings that follow, "open opportunities for us to lament creation's broken condition," and our lament participates in God's own pathos and lament (cf. Romans 8:18–27; quoting Gombis, *Mark*, 191).

DISABILITY

Let's return to the work of Louise Gosbel and what she wrote about defining disability: a disability "is not simply that an individual lives with a particular health condition or impairment, but it is also the resultant impact this condition has on an individual's ability to function within society, including any experience or marginalization or stigmatization associated with the health condition or impairment" (Gosbel, "Disability," 228). With this definition let's look at the woman in the middle of this passage.

According to Leviticus 15:19–30 and the rulings that formed on top of that passage, her impairment of perpetual bleeding makes her (1) unfit for the temple and (2) unusual in a community, and any unusual discharge (3) restricts a woman's function in society. Bonnie Bowman Thurston complicates her disability when she writes, "This woman is without a male relative to be her advocate [with Jesus], without financial resources and subject to blood taboo" (Thurston, "Mark," 554). She's surely stigmatized and many then, as in our own day, would wonder if this is not the result of sin or God's judgment, even if they refuse to say anything aloud.

Her flow meant some would not touch her or permit her in their home. Not only was she stigmatized and marginalized, she found no path to healing. Notice she had suffered for twelve years; she "had suffered a great deal under the care of many doctors" and "had spent all she had." Worse, she was getting worse, not better (5:26).

Why not try Jesus? she must have thought when she heard about him. She simply, but courageously, touched him, which made him unclean, and her impairment or affliction was cured (5:27–29; NIV has "freed"). Jesus was a contagion of purity with the powers to purify others. Instead of making him unclean, her touch released his powers that made her clean. Jesus immediately sensed his healing power had gone into action, and asked who it was who touched him. The disciples, loving the intoxicating sensation of being around a celebrity, query how Jesus could talk about someone touching him when this crowd bustles and bumps. The now cured woman falls at his feet in an embodied confession that it was her (5:33). Her fear is lifted when Jesus affirms her faith and tells her to "Go in peace" and "be healthy from your affliction" (McKnight, *The Second Testament*).

Expand your understanding of peace. This woman's healing meant not just a physical peace and not just the peace of temple access, but the peace of full restoration to community life. No more stigma, and the barrier of marginalization got knocked into the sea with those bizarre pigs. A disabled woman became an abled woman, and from that moment on she no doubt had a sensitivity for those who were disabled.

DEATH

The sandwich structure of today's passage tosses the brighter lights on Jairus' daughter. Back on the Galilee side of the sea, that is, to the Jewish side, a synagogue leader approaches

Jesus. Remember that synagogue was a public assembly hall and not a cathedral-like place designed only for sacred worship. Look at the man as a community leader and a leader of the synagogue services. And also look at this Jewish establishment man as one who, unlike some others, finds hope in Jesus. His name is Jairus, and he begs Jesus to enter his home and heal his dying daughter (5:21–23). The middle portion of this sandwich begins by suspending the top portion with "So Jesus went with him" (5:24). Good stories include a setting, a problem-creating tension (dying daughter, desperate father, more to come below), a climactic moment (encountering Jesus as possible healer), suspension (the middle portion of the passage), and resolution (to which we now turn).

The tension of the dying daughter's desperate daddy reaches both a high moment as well as an apparent sad resolution when some people come to Jesus with the news that the young girl has died (5:35). Mark suspended the story so this moment could open up to an astonishing resolution. Overhearing that sad news, Jesus says, "Don't be afraid; just believe" (5:36). His words suddenly return to the tension but also heighten expectations for surprise.

Jesus restricts the surprise to his three closest followers (5:37). The surprise begins with some people stuck in sad news about the girl's death, who ridicule Jesus when he states that the girl is but sleeping (5:38–40). Sleeping was a common Jewish softening and euphemism for death, but here he poses sleeping over against dying.

Jesus now deepens the potential of a surprise by restricting the audience to three followers and a mom and dad. They alone enter into the girl's room, Jesus takes her by the hand, tells her to get up (in Aramaic), and "immediately the girl stood up and began to walk around" (5:40–42). Jesus instructed them to feed her, too, because his version of redemption is holistic. Of course, unlike the previous miracle, everyone is "beside themselves with great ecstasy" (McKnight, *The Second Testament*), so Jesus, ever alert to the conflict in Galilee over his popularity, "gave strict orders not to let anyone know about this" (5:43).

Did you notice that the twelve-year-old girl was born the same year the woman's bleeding began? I had never noticed that until Emerson Powery pointed it out ("Mark," 132).

This surprise of resuscitating a dead body rates at the top of Jesus' mighty miracles, though it is not the only one (cf. John 11:1–16). The challenge of someone actually raising someone else from the dead, whether it is Jesus or not, slows down into two terse questions: It is not about *Can God?*, for God can, but *Did God?*, and the witness of the Gospels is that God did raise both Jairus' daughter and Lazarus, and those two returns to life, which is not the same as the final eternal resurrection, anticipate the mighty act of God in raising Jesus from the dead. So, I look at the resuscitation of this young girl and of Lazarus through the reality of Jesus' resurrection. If God can, and if God did, then God will again!

The stories of Mark 4 and 5 are variations on themes we have already heard. Jesus does mighty acts, the crowds are both amazed and expanding in numbers, and Jesus does what he can to calm the news about him. I can only say *Good luck with that!* When a healer like Jesus does what Jesus does, the word will spread to anyone and everyone with a need. Which intensifies the conflict in Galilee. Which "ends" in the cross. Which is the paradigm for discipleship. All of which loom over the entire Gospel of Mark.

Questions for Reflection and Application

1. What does the sandwich structure help you see in these stories?

2. How does Jesus' restoration of people to their communities help address their disability status?

3. How does Jairus stand in contrast to some other Jewish leaders?

4. How does the context given here help you better understand the story of the bleeding woman?

5. What in your life needs Jesus' resuscitating work?

FOR FURTHER READING

Louise A. Gosbel, "Disability and Paul," in *The Dictionary of Paul and His Letters*, ed. S. McKnight, Lynn H. Cohick, and Nijay K. Gupta (2d ed.; Downers Grove: IVP Academic, 2023), 228–231.

JESUS OF THE CROSS: INVISIBLE TO THE LOCALS

Mark 6:1–6a

¹ Jesus left there and went to his hometown, accompanied by his disciples. ² When the Sabbath came, he began to teach in the synagogue, and many who heard him were amazed.

"Where did this man get these things?" they asked. "What's this wisdom that has been given him? What are these remarkable miracles he is performing?

³ Isn't this the carpenter? Isn't this Mary's son and the brother of James, Joseph, Judas and Simon? Aren't his sisters here with us?" And they took offense at him.

⁴ Jesus said to them, "A prophet is not without honor except in his own town, among his relatives and in his own home." ⁵ He could not do any miracles there, except lay his hands on a few sick people and heal them. ⁶ He was amazed at their lack of faith.

I once applied for an advanced degree to a university and was rejected, but the professor in charge told me I could call him to talk about why I was rejected. So I did. The professor was kind, clear, and inflexible. This was his explanation: "I will not admit anyone into our PhD program who has attended an evangelical seminary. We've had too

many evangelical students turn classrooms into battle zones."
I could here criticize the professor for bias or evangelicals for
being obnoxious. No need for that but there is a need to say
that some connections are never forgotten.

CONNECTIONS

Jesus' connections did not make him special. Locals in the
sleepy village of Nazareth suggest his family was very ordinary.
They say so with a patronizing tone. They never forgot his
connections. They discredit Jesus with two sets of questions:

Where did this man get these things?

What's this wisdom that has been given him?
What are these remarkable miracles he is performing?
Isn't this the carpenter? [better yet, "artisan"]
Isn't this Mary's son and the brother of James, Joseph,
    Judas, and Simon?
Aren't his sisters here with us?

The first set wonders how such an ordinary man can be
teaching such penetrating ideas about the launching of the
kingdom of God and doing such extraordinary acts. The questions all unfold from the first one, which is why I indented
the next five questions.

The Artisan vs. the Scribe

38:31 All these rely on their hands,
    and all are skillful in their own work.
32 Without them no city can be inhabited,

---

and wherever they live they will not go hungry.
Yet they are not sought out for the council of the
people,
³³ nor do they attain eminence in the public
assembly.
They do not sit in the judge's seat,
nor do they understand the decisions of the
courts;
they cannot expound discipline or judgment,
and they are not found among the rulers.
³⁴ But they maintain the fabric of the world,
and their concern is for
How different the one who devotes himself
to the study of the law of the Most High!
³⁹ᐟ¹ They seek out the wisdom of all the ancients
and are concerned with prophecies;
² they preserve the sayings of the famous
and penetrate the subtleties of parables;
³ they seek out the hidden meanings of proverbs
and are at home with the obscurities of
parables.
⁴ They serve among the great
and appear before rulers;
they travel in foreign nations
and learn what is good and evil in the human lot.
⁵ They set their hearts to rise early
to seek the Lord who made them
and to petition the Most High;
they open their mouths in prayer
and ask pardon for their sins

Sirach 38:31–39:5, NRSVue.

---

* Found in Gombis, *Mark*, 194–195.

The issue is the source of what he says and does. The source has two options: from God or from himself. If the former, he's not dismissable. If the latter, he's a self-claiming charlatan. They opt for the latter *because he's a manual laborer, and he's from such an ordinary family*, which forms the second set of questions. It's a kind of *We know this guy. He works with his hands unlike our esteemed teachers. Plus, we know his mother and the stories about her and him.* (The absence of his father indicates perhaps they think he's an illegitimate child.) *We know his named brothers and his (unnamed) sisters.* The number of children, at least six (four brothers, and more than one sister), in such a small village requires that they know who the "father" of his siblings are, and they probably don't buy the story of his miraculous conception, so they drop the name of Joseph.

His connections created a culture of disbelief (6:6) for those in his hometown.

RESTRICTIONS

Disbelief restricts appropriate honor for the Father who has sent the Spirit onto the Son to launch the kingdom. Jesus quotes a boilerplate observation, at least it's well-known in the circles of the prophets: "A prophet is not without honor except in his own town, among his relatives and in his own home" (6:4). He says this because the locals, the ones who know his family is very ordinary, "took offense at him" (6:3). The word translated "took offense" is *skandalizō*, which can be translated "tripped up" (McKnight, *The Second Testament*) and we get the word "scandalize" from this word. They did not see him and, because they could not see him in his ordinariness, they tripped over him and fell down into disbelief. They could not believe he was who he said he was and who others thought he was.

Disbelief not only restricts honoring Jesus for his messianic mission, disbelief also restricts the holistic redemption of the kingdom of God. Faith is not magic, but without faith Jesus' powers are not unleashed. He gives to those who ask, to those who believe and trust and surrender to him. Mark puts it like this: "He was not able there to do any power, except, placing the hands on a few ill ones, he healed" (6:5; Mcknight, *The Second Testament*).

Jesus deserved honor; he deserved trust to do his mighty works. But because of his ordinary family, the locals mostly ignored him. One more indication that Jesus was headed toward the ultimate scandal, the cross, and one more indication that to follow Jesus was to follow a disrespected agent of God. A too-often irony in the history of the church has been that leaders prefer the way of acceptance and glory and, in so choosing such a path, fail to follow Jesus with the fullness of who he is. That God chose him and his story to launch the kingdom makes no sense to most humans. "In the eyes of the world, it is completely backward" (Gombis, *Mark*, 198).

QUESTIONS FOR REFLECTION AND APPLICATION

1. How does reading about Jesus' family connections help humanize him?

2. What suspicions did people display about Jesus' upbringing?

3. How does people's belief interact with Jesus' power?

4. In what ways does Jesus contrast with many popular Christian leaders today?

5. How do you think Jesus might have felt about being judged, shamed, and rejected by those who knew him and his family?

JESUS OF THE CROSS: MISSION IN THE SHADOW OF JOHN

Mark 6:6b–30

⁶ᵇ Then Jesus went around teaching from village to village. ⁷ Calling the Twelve to him, he began to send them out two by two and gave them authority over impure spirits.

⁸ These were his instructions: "Take nothing for the journey except a staff—no bread, no bag, no money in your belts. ⁹ Wear sandals but not an extra shirt. ¹⁰ Whenever you enter a house, stay there until you leave that town. ¹¹ And if any place will not welcome you or listen to you, leave that place and shake the dust off your feet as a testimony against them."

¹² They went out and preached that people should repent. ¹³ They drove out many demons and anointed many sick people with oil and healed them.

¹⁴ King Herod heard about this, for Jesus' name had become well known. Some were saying, "John the Baptist has been raised from the dead, and that is why miraculous powers are at work in him."

¹⁵ Others said, "He is Elijah."

And still others claimed, "He is a prophet, like one of the prophets of long ago."

[16] But when Herod heard this, he said, "John, whom I beheaded, has been raised from the dead!"

[17] For Herod himself had given orders to have John arrested, and he had him bound and put in prison. He did this because of Herodias, his brother Philip's wife, whom he had married. [18] For John had been saying to Herod, "It is not lawful for you to have your brother's wife." [19] So Herodias nursed a grudge against John and wanted to kill him. But she was not able to, [20] because Herod feared John and protected him, knowing him to be a righteous and holy man. When Herod heard John, he was greatly puzzled; yet he liked to listen to him.

[21] Finally the opportune time came. On his birthday Herod gave a banquet for his high officials and military commanders and the leading men of Galilee. [22] When the daughter of Herodias came in and danced, she pleased Herod and his dinner guests.

The king said to the girl, "Ask me for anything you want, and I'll give it to you."

[23] And he promised her with an oath, "Whatever you ask I will give you, up to half my kingdom."

[24] She went out and said to her mother, "What shall I ask for?"

"The head of John the Baptist," she answered.

[25] At once the girl hurried in to the king with the request: "I want you to give me right now the head of John the Baptist on a platter."

[26] The king was greatly distressed, but because of his oaths and his dinner guests, he did not want to refuse her. [27] So he immediately sent an executioner with orders to bring John's head. The man went, beheaded John in the prison, [28] and brought back his head on a platter. He presented it to the girl,

and she gave it to her mother. ²⁹ *On hearing of this, John's disciples came and took his body and laid it in a tomb.*

³⁰ *The apostles gathered around Jesus and reported to him all they had done and taught.*

Today's passage is another Markan sandwich structure. Jesus sends the twelve out, then in a flashback in history Mark recounts the hedonistic, barbaric decapitation of John the Baptist, and then the twelve return. Their mission then frames the potential implication of speaking truth to power and of following the Jesus of the Cross. Tim Gombis cleverly understates the passage, writing that "Mark indicates that disciples of Jesus are not guaranteed a soft and easy life," but then immediately notes their lives may encounter "dangerously threatening circumstances" (Gombis, *Mark*, 200). Put into a formula, the Jesus of the Cross implies disciples of the Cross. I will begin with the middle portion (visible above by indentation) and then move to the frames.

Mission work that extends and expands the ministry of Jesus cuts against the grain of so much of the evangelism and missionary enterprises in our world today. In fact, evangelism has become a four-letter word for many. Whether we like what is said or not, few would deny the diminishment of an evangelistic impulse in much of the church today. Long ago Lesslie Newbigin mentioned the problems with evangelism. What he said in India decades ago remains accurate. He mentions confusing evangelism with proselytizing people into our own church or group, the manipulative methods of some, our come-and-go approach instead of being with and living among those to whom we want to minister, the use of commercial sales techniques, and the distortion of the gospel, which has become how-to-get-into-heaven-when-we-die instead of summoning people to follow Jesus with us (Newbigin, *Good Shepherd*, 59–60). I could go on. We can latch onto his third point and drill down into Mark's Gospel and today's passage. That is, when people become authentic witnesses of Jesus by embodying in a life that counts, as Jesus' did, then our gospel work will avoid these pitfalls and look far more like the mission of these apostles.

But First . . .

Before turning to the passage, we need to recognize the barbarity of the scene in the middle of this passage. In recognizing the barbarity, however, we tend to pass over this scene as simply part of the story of John the Baptist and we move on. John was made in God's image and was precious to God. Herod Antipas was not technically a "king" (Mark 6:14), and both Matthew and Luke give him his proper title, *tetrarch* (Matthew 14:1; Luke 9:7). He was in the mood of retaliation for his brother (Herod Philip), and as a result of a hedonistic dance, a dance of his sister-in-law's daughter, offers her whatever she wants up to half the kingdom. That long complicated sentence has enough in it for us to see the decapitation for what it was: a sickening display of barbarous exploitation of power for the sheer whim of it. Sure, it bothered him. The point however is that we need to pause over such descriptions, not as short rest stops on our way to Jerusalem but as an example (1) of what God never wants for humans or against humans, and (2) of the capacity for humans to enact heinous murders.

Violence needs to be seen for what it is. In my early twenties I was with a group of summer missionaries in Austria. Near the end of our trip, we were taken to Mauthausen, a small concentration camp in Austria. There I observed pictures of barbaric cruelty, including reading a sign about the day some in the camp were told to pick blueberries. The deception was that they would become victims of a mass shooting and buried as a group in a ditch. It was there that the Holocaust penetrated my being, and from that day on I have been both attracted to the truth of such violence and repelled by its vicious inhumanity. Let's pause to consider if we are taking stock of the violence of this scene. Violence like this leads us to lament.

THE BAPTIST SPEAKS TRUTH TO POWER

When Herod the Great died, his kingdom was passed on to his sons, including Antipas who ruled in Galilee and Perea, and Philip who ruled in the northeastern portion of Herod's kingdom. Philip married Herodias, Philip's brother's former wife. John the Baptist knew this was against the law of the land. Somehow he addressed Herod Antipas and protested the marriage. Knowing how John had preached along the Jordan and how he demanded repentance (see Matthew 3:7–11), it is more than likely that John let Antipas have it with vitriol and warning of divine judgment (Mark 6:18). Herodias despised John. Antipas feared John's prophetic gifts, that is, that he was "a righteous and godly man" and so "protected him." Antipas was himself in tension of John: he was both "greatly puzzled" and "yet he liked to listen to him" (6:20). Many politicians with power like to have religious experts around, not only because it soothes a troubled conscience, but also because it persuades the crowds of the supposed sanctity of the politician.

The tensions pitched at a lusty event in which Herodias' daughter danced and "pleased Herod and his dinner guests" (6:22; notice Genesis 19:8; Judges 14:1, 3, 7). His reckless request for anything she wanted turns into a prophetic embarrassment, or as Mark phrases it, "the king was greatly distressed" but decided to honor his word as he dishonored a prophet he feared (Mark 6:26). In Machaerus, the prison, John was beheaded. The height of barbarity is the presentation of the head on a platter to the girl, who gives it to her vindictive mother (6:28–29). The tragic murder of John finishes with his own disciples caring for his body and laying it in a tomb (6:29).

The death of John is, as Emerson Powery writes, the "end of the innocence of Jesus' mission" (Powery, "Mark," 133). Mark tells this story in a manner that reveals that the lives of Jesus and his missioners were at stake in their mission. This event foreshadows the Cross. Their connection to Jesus, and his connection to John, means their relationship to Jesus puts them in jeopardy with Philip and Herodias, if not Antipas. Rome, in other words, is breathing down their necks. As Rome would on Jesus when crucified. This incident tosses shade on the entire ministry of Jesus, and the conflict in Galilee begins to look even more sinister. Speaking truth to power, which John had done and which Jesus would do, requires a person to face what could happen. For Jesus it means a cross, not decapitation. For the disciples, it will mean various forms of opposition, persecution, and for Peter, crucified upside down in Rome (according to tradition).

THE DISCIPLES DO GOSPEL WORK

Jesus' public ministry, in its tension between publicity and withdrawing, led to a strategy of distributing the kingdom ministry gifts to twelve apostles (3:13–19), but they are not recorded as being sent out to do that ministry until Mark's sixth chapter. Jesus sent them out "two by two," distributing his power to them to have "authority over impure spirits" (6:7). He sent them into surrounding villages in Galilee, knowing they'd not return that day. So he gave them instructions that were shaped by a desire not to appear as if they were doing it for money (6:8–9) and not to move from house to house in a desire to get to the nicest homes in the community (6:10). As God provided miraculously for the children of Israel (Exodus 16; Deuteronomy 8:4; 29:5–6), so God would prompt locals to provide food and shelter for the missioners (Gombis, *Mark*, 201). And Jesus instructed them to use a symbolic action made famous by Israel's prophets. If "any place" rejects the kingdom mission, they were to "shake the dust off [their] feet as a testimony against them" (6:11). They did more than exorcise demons. They "preached that people should repent" like John (1:4) and Jesus (1:15). Mark does not tell us they preached the kingdom but that's implied in repentance (as at 1:15). Their missions were successful (6:13).

So successful they acquired like Jesus a following and publicity. The news got to Antipas who did his best to interpret the news. His best was not accurate. He figured the man he beheaded had come back to life, while others, perhaps knowing of those prophet-like actions, connected the disciples to Elijah, who also was thought by some to be someone who would return. Antipas preferred his own interpretation and chalked it up to John (6:14–16). Then Mark tells us all about John the Baptist, Philip, and Herodias (6:17–29).

With decapitation as the end for John's speaking truth to power, the return of the twelve and their report sounds like little more than a debriefing (6:30). But Mark's framing will not let us skim the verse. Their debriefing for those reading this Gospel entails a prospect of not just opposition to the gospel work but the reality of the kind of opposition that ends in martyrdom. Their mission surrounds a decapitation of a relative of Jesus, a witness of the kingdom, a fearless prophet speaking truth to power.

To frame this all by Mark's own Gospel, the Jesus of

the Cross and the John of the platter form the paradigm of the disciples of the Cross. To follow Jesus puts one's life at stake. Not so much for many today because of the growth of the gospel in the world, making it a part of culture, but also because of laws of free speech in many countries. But there are plenty of locations today where witnesses to the kingdom of Jesus entails opposition, persecution, and martyrdom.

QUESTIONS FOR REFLECTION AND APPLICATION

1. How can Mark's Gospel help us become good witnesses for Jesus who avoid many of the pitfalls of modern "evangelism"?

2. When you pause to consider this story of John the Baptist, what strikes you about it?

3. What impact do you think John's murder had on Jesus' disciples?

4. What might it look like for you to "shake the dust off your feet" in places that refuse to receive kingdom ministry from you?

5. Greater acceptance of Christianity in culture and free speech laws have made persecution less likely in some parts of the world, but what opposition might you face as you follow Jesus?

FOR FURTHER READING

Lesslie Newbigin, *The Good Shepherd: Meditations on Christian Ministry in Today's World* (Grand Rapids: Wm. B. Eerdmans, 1977).

JESUS OF THE CROSS: PROVISIONS ON THE WAY

Mark 6:31–44

³¹ Then, because so many people were coming and going that they did not even have a chance to eat, he said to them, "Come with me by yourselves to a quiet place and get some rest." ³² So they went away by themselves in a boat to a solitary place. ³³ But many who saw them leaving recognized them and ran on foot from all the towns and got there ahead of them. ³⁴ When Jesus landed and saw a large crowd, he had compassion on them, because they were like sheep without a shepherd. So he began teaching them many things.

³⁵ By this time it was late in the day, so his disciples came to him. "This is a remote place," they said, "and it's already very late. ³⁶ Send the people away so that they can go to the surrounding countryside and villages and buy themselves something to eat."

³⁷ But he answered, "You give them something to eat."

They said to him, "That would take more than half a year's wages! Are we to go and spend that much on bread and give it to them to eat?"

³⁸ "How many loaves do you have?" he asked. "Go and see."

When they found out, they said, "Five—and two fish."

³⁹ Then Jesus directed them to have all the people sit down

in groups on the green grass. [40] So they sat down in groups of hundreds and fifties. [41] Taking the five loaves and the two fish and looking up to heaven, he gave thanks and broke the loaves. Then he gave them to his disciples to distribute to the people. He also divided the two fish among them all. [42] They all ate and were satisfied, [43] and the disciples picked up twelve basketfuls of broken pieces of bread and fish. [44] The number of the men who had eaten was five thousand.

When Kris and I were in England and I was working on an advanced degree at the University of Nottingham, we were going by faith. It was a bit of a risk, and somehow God was prompting others to help us along. One evening, in the first year we were there, someone knocked on the door and I opened to be startled to see our pastor. I wondered what we, the Americans, had done. He asked if he could come in; he did and quickly informed us that he had heard our funds would not last for the entirety of the degree. Then he offered to pay for our expenses until we could return home. He said that we can pay him back for as long as it would take. When we got back, I began teaching, and we saved and scrimped to pay him back for his generosity. I'm writing these lines, so I believe, only because of God's provisions through that generous church leader. God prompted him to risk paying for us.

You may have a story of God's provisions too. Perhaps today's passage will remind you of those provisions, and perhaps too it will prompt you to provide for someone else. As the pastor prompted us to provide for others in the last four decades. Our passage speaks to two sorts of provisions each of us needs in the kingdom mission, rest and food. The first provision is for the agents of the kingdom mission, the apostles, and the second for the populace, the crowds whom Jesus wanted to gather into the kingdom. This passage makes clear just how large the following of Jesus is becoming. A crowd of five thousand men, which would mean over 10,000 total, would concern the temple authorities if it were to become known in Jerusalem and, if it got to Antipas or Pilate, would be in the scope of Rome.

FROM REST TO NO REST
IN THE MISSION

Our passage begins with the business of life, saying, "because so many were coming and going that they did not even have a chance to eat" (6:31). The busy-ness ratio in our life, what some call the "lack of margin," has escalated at the same time the Western world's income and the availability of leisure time have risen! There's hardly a day that goes by that someone doesn't write to me with this kind of opening: "I know you are a busy man, but . . .". That opening just as often is telling me how busy that person is.

We need rest, we need a Sabbath-principle, we need to tune the busy-ness and the rush to accomplish more down. Jesus knew the harried life a kingdom mission could generate, and he saw it in the faces of his twelve apostles when they returned. So he sought with them "a quiet place" where they could "get some rest" (6:31). Quiet means time to concentrate on what we need to concentrate on, or it means silence and stillness—a calm lake, a cozy chair, a warm room, a place to veg. Rest restores body, soul, mind, and heart.

They all get into a boat and head for a "solitary place," or more literally, "a wilderness place," until people discovered their hiding place! It is not uncommon for those on mission to have their lives interrupted by people in need of gospel care, and the needs are as varied as the people are different. Just ask anyone who ministers to people in need.

FROM NEGLECT TO COMPASSION IN THE MISSION

Jesus perceives the first need as pastoral care. The people—and here we have the crowds—thousands—that have figured so often in the Gospel of Mark—are "like sheep without a shepherd" (6:34). That expression criticizes the lack of care by the temple agents who want to be the leaders of the crowds in Galilee. The need here is "teaching them many things" (6:34). Many people were invisible and neglected by leaders, and Jesus' mission was to make the invisible visible and the neglected cared for. Because the need is great, Jesus sends agents to spread pastoral care to the ones in need of compassion.

Jesus became famous for his compassion for the needy, and passage after passage in the Gospel of Mark already illustrated his healings and exorcisms. One should not suppose that the most exclusive forms of Judaism represent what was at work in Galilee, but what is clear is that Jesus perceived pastoral neglect. Here is a text from an exclusivist sect, the Essenes of Qumran, who set out clear restrictions for who could be in their angel-superintended *yahad*, or congregation or community.

> [13b] Everything that is revealed from the Law for the multitude of the [14] Camp, and in which he (the postulant) has imperfect knowledge, the Overseer should tell him and command him to study [15] for one full year; and then according to his knowledge he may draw near. But no one who is a fool or insane may enter; and no simpleton or ignoramus [16] or one with eyes too weak to see or lame or crippled or deaf or minor child, [17] none of these shall enter the congregation, for the holy angels are in your midst (CD 15:13b–17).

Again, please don't think the leaders of Galilee excluded people this rigorously. But please do assume that for many people those who are non-normative or disabled are knocked down on the social status ladder. They can become the first to be ignored, invisible, and neglected. Jesus had the gift of finding the ignored.

Pastoral care takes shape in many forms, including providing rest, teaching, and food. The skill of spotting the invisible and discovering those on the margins percolates up and out of patient listening, prayer, and questioning the systems in place. The kingdom mission of Jesus is a holistic redemption mission, and what is needed will vary from person to person, from time to time, and from location to location. Some churches provide winter coats for folks in the community, others provide day care or after school care, others provide society for singles, others open up a soup kitchen or a pantry, while others specialize in visitations with the lonely and seniors. Compassion flows from sensitivity in specific contexts.

FROM NO FOOD TO FOOD IN THE MISSION

Near dinner time the disciples of Jesus realized people were a distance from their homes and they had not anticipated, when leaving to be with Jesus, that they'd need food. So the disciples asked Jesus to send folks home and, to borrow a current trope in the news, "end the revival" so people could eat. Surely the disciples perceived themselves extending Jesus' own compassion for others in thinking of their need to get home.

Not Jesus. He saw them failing to act in compassion. He instructs them to feed them, and you know the drill: they don't have that much food, they discover five loaves of bread and two fishes, and Jesus turns that meal for a small family into a meal for a massive following. This, too, is a nature miracle (p. 71). The abundance of leftovers establishes the abundance of God's provision, and it outdoes by far the manna miracle of Exodus 16. We will find another instance like this in Mark 8:1–10, and we have discussed such feeding miracles in both *Luke* and *John*, in this Everyday Bible Study series.

God provides, and very rarely are the provisions miracles, especially nature miracles. But in providing rest, in providing fellowship with others, in providing food and shelter through fellow companions on the kingdom mission, God is at work to provide what people need. Agents of Jesus are called to join God in the great work of care, compassion, and provision.

QUESTIONS FOR REFLECTION AND APPLICATION

1. Can you think of a time when God miraculously provided for you, or God helped you provide for someone else?

2. When have you experienced exceptional pastoral care that reminded you of Jesus?

3. When have pastors neglected or mistreated you?

4. Would you call this miraculous feeding a "nature miracle" or make up a different category?

5. Where do you like to go to find solitude and rest?

FOR FURTHER READING

On Jewish texts of exclusion, see Cecilia Wassen, "What Do Angels Have against the Blind and Deaf? Rules of Exclusion in the Dead Sea Scrolls," in *Common Judaism: Explorations in Second-Temple Judaism* (ed. Wayne O. McCready and Adele Reinhartz; Minneapolis: Fortress, 2008), pp. 115–129.

JESUS OF THE CROSS: CROWDS AND DISCIPLES

Mark 6:45–56

⁴⁵ Immediately Jesus made his disciples get into the boat and go on ahead of him to Bethsaida, while he dismissed the crowd. ⁴⁶ After leaving them, he went up on a mountainside to pray.

⁴⁷ Later that night, the boat was in the middle of the lake, and he was alone on land. ⁴⁸ He saw the disciples straining at the oars, because the wind was against them. Shortly before dawn he went out to them, walking on the lake. He was about to pass by them, ⁴⁹ but when they saw him walking on the lake, they thought he was a ghost. They cried out, ⁵⁰ because they all saw him and were terrified.

Immediately he spoke to them and said, "Take courage! It is I. Don't be afraid."

⁵¹ Then he climbed into the boat with them, and the wind died down. They were completely amazed, ⁵² for they had not understood about the loaves; their hearts were hardened.

⁵³ When they had crossed over, they landed at Gennesaret and anchored there. ⁵⁴ As soon as they got out of the boat, people

recognized Jesus. [55] *They ran throughout that whole region and carried the sick on mats to wherever they heard he was.* [56] *And wherever he went—into villages, towns or countryside—they placed the sick in the marketplaces. They begged him to let them touch even the edge of his cloak, and all who touched it were healed.*

Not all see it, but today's passage is another Markan sandwich (see formatting above). The top and bottom layer of the sandwich are about crowds, and the middle portion is about Jesus revealing more of his glory to the disciples. What the crowds see is not what the disciples see, but the disciples at times seem to perceive little more than the crowds.

START HERE

The most important lines in today's passage can be found in Mark 6:51–52: "They were completely amazed, for they had not understood about the loaves; their hearts were hardened." Jesus just fed thousands in a miracle exceeding all but the raising of the young girl from death. Mark does not commend the disciples in saying they were "terrified" (6:50) and then "greatly, aboundingly beside themselves" (6:52; McKnight, *The Second Testament*) when they realize Jesus walked on water. In fact, Mark assigns their fear to not understanding what had been revealed about God's powers in the loaves. Then Mark tells us "their hearts were hardened," which sounds like the story about Pharaoh, his magicians, and the work of God through Moses and Aaron (Exodus 7:13). God's revelation and a human's lack of response interact to form the Bible's sense of hardheartedness. It would be morally wrong for God to harden someone's heart and then blame them for not responding. I like to see the expression about hard-heartedness in the disciples as a negative way of saying their hearts were slowly, and only slowly, softening.

We begin with this then: the disciples just didn't get it.

THE CROWDS

You may be surprised to read here that the disciples didn't get it, but they got more than the crowds but not enough to grip the Water Walker's power not only to provide but also to protect. Faith in the first three Gospels has three senses: *pistis, oligopistia, apistia.* Faith, little faith, anti- or no faith. The disciples of Jesus have embraced Jesus in faith but in the exercise of their faith they at times struggled to live out what they believed. The crowds never seem to get beyond an embrace of Jesus and a fascination with him. Opponents of Jesus are those with anti-faith or no faith. The irony of these three terms is that *oligopistia*, which looks like someone with barely any faith, is actually a step beyond *pistis*. Only those with faith can be accused of little faith. As Frederick Buechner said once, faith is "on-again-off-again rather than once-and-for-all. Faith is not being sure where you're going, but going anyway" (Buechner, *Beyond Words*, 109).

Jesus dismisses the crowds to retire onto a "mountainside to pray" (6:45). This is part of the withdrawal theme in Mark, one of Jesus' strategies for managing the problem of publicity. With the crowds out of the way, Jesus reveals himself on the water *but only to the disciples*. Because they know Jesus as the healer of all ills, they gather around him and can turn Jesus into a spectacle. Which is the impression one gets in the bottom layer of this sandwich (6:53–56).

The disciples, with Jesus joining them, boated out of Bethsaida into the Sea of Galilee and then returned to "Gennesaret," and geographers have been perplexed by the locations. Bethsaida and Gennesaret, which is a plain near Capernaum, are close to one another.

THE WATER WALKER IS
THE WIND RAKER

The crowds adore Jesus, the disciples are following Jesus, but they, fighting a contrary wind and waves swamping the boat, are challenged to see if the Food Distributor can protect and save them. The middle portion of this Markan sandwich reveals the Water Walker who deserves a deeper faith on the part of the disciples. I've been on the Sea of Galilee in a windy, wavy rainstorm. I was not in a first century boat but a twenty-first century boat. Nor were we rowing. The disciples were probably grumbling with one another when, totally unexpected, they see Jesus "walking around on the Sea" (6:48; McKnight, *The Second Testament*). The word translated "walking" in the NIV is a word often used for walking around. One could be forgiven for thinking Jesus was out for a stroll, of course with a purpose.

The oddest expression was Jesus "was about to pass them by," as if he was not out there to come to their rescue. In fact, the language "pass them by" evokes God's passing by Moses when revealing to him the divine glory (Exodus 33:17–34:7). Mark's description should not be skipped over: the passing them by theme reveals Jesus as the glory of God. Though the disciples do recognize the Water Walker as Jesus, their faith had failed to their fear. Jesus responds to their cries with words of assurance, "Take courage!" which is followed not by "It is I" (NIV) but with "I am" as in the Gospel of John's famous "I am" sayings (see McKnight, *John*, 103). When we add the passing by to the I am statement we calculate a revelation of the deity of Jesus being revealed. The Water Walker is the Food Distributor, God incarnate, who, now entering into the boat with the disciples, becomes the Wind Raker.

They are "amazed" at Jesus but being amazed is not enough for our author. Mark knows they had not formed the kind of faith that knows the Food Distributer can be the Wind Raker. But, as I have said already, their faith was challenged in a way the crowds had not yet experienced.

Following Jesus summons us to infer from who Jesus is to trust in the way of Jesus, regardless of the cost. The winds on the Sea call a follower of Jesus to deny oneself and trust in God as well as that they anticipate the ultimate wind of martyrdom. The Cross of Jesus calls the followers to be disciples of the Cross. Jesus is with us even when we don't know it and when his very presence terrifies us, and he can calm the wind.

QUESTIONS FOR REFLECTION AND APPLICATION

1. Why did the disciples not yet understand Jesus and what he was up to?

2. What are some strategies you have seen Jesus use so far in Mark for dealing with the crowds?

3. How does this passage reveal important markers of Jesus' identity?

4. Walter Brueggemann calls our attention to echoes of Isaiah in the "I am" and in the "do not fear" expressions: notice Isaiah 42:6; 43:11, 25; 44:6, 24; 45:5 and Isaiah 41:10, 13; 43:1, 5; 44:8. How do these verses in Isaiah help us understand the disciples in the boat? (Brueggemann, *Sermons*, 147)

5. What in your life needs Jesus' wind-calming work?

FOR FURTHER READING

Walter Brueggemann, *The Collected Sermons of Walter Brueggemann* (Louisville: Westminster John Knox, 2011).

Frederick Buechner, *Beyond Words: Daily Readings in the ABC's of Faith* (San Francisco: HarperSanFrancisco, 2004).

Scot McKnight, Everyday Bible Study: *John* (Grand Rapids: HarperChristian Resources, 2022).

JESUS OF THE CROSS: CONSERVATIVE JESUS

Mark 7:1–23

¹ The Pharisees and some of the teachers of the law who had come from Jerusalem gathered around Jesus ² and saw some of his disciples eating food with hands that were defiled, that is, unwashed. ³ (The Pharisees and all the Jews do not eat unless they give their hands a ceremonial washing, holding to the tradition of the elders. ⁴ When they come from the marketplace they do not eat unless they wash. And they observe many other traditions, such as the washing of cups, pitchers and kettles.)

⁵ So the Pharisees and teachers of the law asked Jesus, "Why don't your disciples live according to the tradition of the elders instead of eating their food with defiled hands?"

⁶ He replied, "Isaiah was right when he prophesied about you hypocrites; as it is written:

> These people honor me with their lips,
>   but their hearts are far from me.
> ⁷ They worship me in vain;
>   their teachings are merely human rules.'

⁸ *You have let go of the commands of God and are holding on to human traditions."*

⁹ *And he continued, "You have a fine way of setting aside the commands of God in order to observe your own traditions!* ¹⁰ *For Moses said, 'Honor your father and mother,' and, 'Anyone who curses their father or mother is to be put to death.'* ¹¹ *But you say that if anyone declares that what might have been used to help their father or mother is Corban (that is, devoted to God)—*¹² *then you no longer let them do anything for their father or mother.* ¹³ *Thus you nullify the word of God by your tradition that you have handed down. And you do many things like that."*

¹⁴ *Again Jesus called the crowd to him and said, "Listen to me, everyone, and understand this.* ¹⁵ *Nothing outside a person can defile them by going into them. Rather, it is what comes out of a person that defiles them."**

¹⁷ *After he had left the crowd and entered the house, his disciples asked him about this parable.* ¹⁸ *"Are you so dull?" he asked. "Don't you see that nothing that enters a person from the outside can defile them?* ¹⁹ *For it doesn't go into their heart but into their stomach, and then out of the body." (In saying this, Jesus declared all foods clean.)*

²⁰ *He went on: "What comes out of a person is what defiles them.* ²¹ *For it is from within, out of a person's heart, that evil thoughts come—sexual immorality, theft, murder,* ²² *adultery, greed, malice, deceit, lewdness, envy, slander, arrogance and folly.* ²³ *All these evils come from inside and defile a person."*

Now don't mutter bad things about me when you read what I write next. In today's passage Jesus is the conservative and the Pharisees and their buddies, law experts, are the progressives. I don't mean to pat either of today's political

---

* Some manuscripts have here what is found now at Mark 4:23, "If anyone has ears to hear, let them hear."

groups on the back by composing a meme about who's conservative and who's progressive. Instead, this passage, when read well, sets Jesus and the Pharisees into a first century context. In that context the Pharisees and friends have added to the law and made it more practicable while Jesus wants to go back to the Bible and the Bible alone. In that context also are disciples who both don't comprehend the significance of Jesus' feeding miracle or his teachings. In Mark's Gospel the disciples are only on the way in faith; they are not full of faith.

In today's passage the Pharisees and law experts are described poking at Jesus because his disciples aren't following a conventional interpretation of handwashing before eating. It reminds me of my high school and college days when one was inspected over whether one prayed before a meal at a restaurant. (A friend told me in his church one needed to pray only if the meal cost over $1.00.) Then Jesus responds to them; then the disciples need some explanation for what Jesus was getting at.

WHY DO THE DISCIPLES NOT FOLLOW OUR CONVENTIONS?

Two groups, the first a group famous for their confession of Torah observance and the second for their profession as scribes, overlap in important ways. Both are mostly dependent for income on the temple system in Jerusalem. Together they are influential with the populace. Notice these two groups "had come from Jerusalem" (7:1). They are agents of the temple authorities and are in Galilee to inspect Jesus. The entire passage, then, speaks into the conflict over Jesus and his kingdom mission, now expanding with the apostles as agents.

The Pharisees and experts "saw" that "some of his disciples" were eating food with "defiled" or "unwashed" hands. The law does not require a rite for washing one's hands before eating. In fact, Mark says "all the Jews" have expanded purifying rites that include "washing cups, pitchers and kettles" (7:2–4). Purity laws like this intensified the laws about foods faithful Jews could and could not eat. (For a good example, read Acts 10:9–23.) The word for handwashing describes one cupping a hand, filling it with water, and then pouring out the water from one cupped hand to another—which streams through the fingers onto the backhand—and this constitutes a properly washed hand. These practices concern what is clean vs. what is unclean. Such purity practices made a person fit for temple worship. It is clear that the Pharisees and experts thought observant, devout Jews ought to live in a way that makes one always fit for the temple. What is clean however is not technically a moral issue but a ritual, ceremonial, fit-for-the-temple issue. One could become unclean—through touching something unclean— quite often. What Judaism expected was for the person to purify oneself by following laws of purification, like entering into a purifying pool (*mikveh*), and these pools are found in the archaeological sites of ancient villages in Galilee.

Clean and Holy

These two terms are not synonyms, though do overlap at times. Think of these terms, when applied to a human, this way:

- Clean = fit for presence and acts in the temple.
- Holy = fit for the presence of God; devoted to the God who is holy.
- Clean and unclean correspond to pure and common (or impure).

The observant group queries Jesus about why his disciples don't follow the conventions of their interpretation of how best to follow the law. Notice that their conventions are not in the law but are based on the law. A group's interpretation or convention is, however, nearly indistinguishable from the law for that group because those who don't follow that convention are not in the group, and therefore in some sense unobservant.

BECAUSE THEY FOLLOW MY TEACHINGS

Asking Jesus a question can be fraught with potential responses, not all of them comforting. Jesus offers three responses. First, he quotes the Bible against them, that is, he cites Isaiah 29:13's famous words against Jerusalem's inadequate religion. What they say is not the same as their heart; their worship is vain because their "teachings are merely human rules" (Mark 7:6–7). Quoting the Bible against those who think they are the most committed to the Bible raises the stakes.

Second, Jesus contends their conventions subvert the "commands of God" (7:8–13). He illustrates this point. A command is to honor mother and father, but their convention called "Corban," or something given to God or dedicated to the temple, and thus is holy or sacred, exempts that item from being used to help one's parents in the public realm. It should be noted here that this puts the Pharisees in favor with the temple authorities because the gift financially supports the temple. One does not have to be a cynic to think someone could create a convention to favor the temple in order to be empowered by the temple.

Third, Jesus criticizes their meaning of purity by internalizing purity. Purity, like handwashing, occurs to the body but Jesus makes purity as "what comes out of a person" (7:15). Jesus does not here dismiss common acts of purity, which both are taught in the Bible (Leviticus 11) would be necessary for ordinary Jewish life and especially participation in the temple at the major festivals. Rather, he intensifies purity by making it both an inner and outer reality. Again, Jesus is not teaching something that would not have been known in the Jewish world, but he is emphasizing an inner reality in a way that degrades the conventions of the Pharisees and experts. In fact, Jesus here enters into a debate on a common Jewish basis. Again, what Jesus teaches is not forcing a choice: either handwashing or internal purity. He is emphasizing internal purity as more important. So, he forces in this debate with fellow observant Jews. Where does the emphasis in Scripture land?

Jesus' teachings then counter the growing and expanding conventions of the Pharisees and experts. He appeals to Scripture, both explicitly and in a theology of inner purity. He is not against washing hands. Instead, his vision is called a center-set: get the most important thing right, one's inner life, and it will take care of the outer life. It is an inner toward outer, not an inner vs. outer, mindset.

And, by the Way, Purity Begins Inside

Over and over in Mark's Gospel the disciples are right next to Jesus, but they are not swift enough to stay with his teachings. So they ask questions, and again, asking Jesus a question leads often to a reprimand instruction. He chides them with a question: "Are you so dull?" (7:18). Then he largely repeats what he said in 7:15. Food that enters the body, washed hands or not, is a material reality that enters and then exits the body. What seems undeniable is that Mark contends in his own form of a sidebar or block quote that "Jesus declared all foods clean" (7:19). This is hard to square with the food laws of Leviticus 11. The inner world, where genuine purity is to be found, contaminates a person when it produces "evil thoughts" and practices, and Jesus mentions "sexual immorality, theft, murder, adultery, greed, malice, deceit, lewdness, envy, slander, arrogance and folly" (7:21–22).

The only instruction left is not stated but implied: so purify the heart by turning yourself over to God, get baptized, and follow the Jesus of the Cross. Jesus' sense of purity transcends that of the Pharisees and experts. The unclean who touched him he was able to purify, so that Jesus himself became an agent of purity. That is, he was a walking contagion of purity. The internal purity he teaches derives from a person's relationship to Jesus the Purifier.

QUESTIONS FOR REFLECTION AND APPLICATION

1. What do the Torah authorities and scribes have in common?

2. Why do you think purity rules were important in Jesus' time and culture?

3. On what basis does Jesus criticize his opponents?

4. Can you name some interpretations of the New Testament that have become nearly equivalent to the New Testament in your church, denomination, or tradition?

5. How would you say "purity" and "clean" are defined in your Christian community?

JESUS OF THE CROSS: KINGDOM POWER FOR ALL

Mark 7:24–37

24 Jesus left that place and went to the vicinity of Tyre. He entered a house and did not want anyone to know it; yet he could not keep his presence secret. 25 In fact, as soon as she heard about him, a woman whose little daughter was possessed by an impure spirit came and fell at his feet. 26 The woman was a Greek, born in Syrian Phoenicia. She begged Jesus to drive the demon out of her daughter.

27 "First let the children eat all they want," he told her, "for it is not right to take the children's bread and toss it to the dogs."

28 "Lord," she replied, "even the dogs under the table eat the children's crumbs."

29 Then he told her, "For such a reply, you may go; the demon has left your daughter."

30 She went home and found her child lying on the bed, and the demon gone.

31Then Jesus left the vicinity of Tyre and went through Sidon, down to the Sea of Galilee and into the region of the Decapolis. 32 There some people brought to him a man who was deaf and could hardly talk, and they begged Jesus to place his hand on him.

³³ *After he took him aside, away from the crowd, Jesus put his fingers into the man's ears. Then he spit and touched the man's tongue.* ³⁴ *He looked up to heaven and with a deep sigh said to him, "Ephphatha!" (which means "Be opened!"). * ³⁵ *At this, the man's ears were opened, his tongue was loosened and he began to speak plainly.*

³⁶ *Jesus commanded them not to tell anyone. But the more he did so, the more they kept talking about it.* ³⁷ *People were overwhelmed with amazement. "He has done everything well," they said. "He even makes the deaf hear and the mute speak."*

Sometimes it's best to walk away. The person who walks away, however, takes her gifts, her skills, and her personality with her. Which means, if the person is one with ministry gifts, she will walk right into other people to whom she can minister. When Beth Moore, whose new autobiography is running up the bestseller charts, left her Baptist church and went to another church, that church quickly surrounded her with those who look to experience her undeniable gifts of teaching and speaking (Moore, *All My Knotted-Up Life*). Just like Jesus. The two episodes in today's passage reveal that (1) Jesus has to walk away (literally) from his kingdom work in Galilee and (2) that Jesus uses kingdom power for persons in need outside Galilee. As Emerson Powery observes, it's a small step from all foods are clean (7:19) to all persons can be cleansed (7:24–37; Powery, "Mark," 135). In fact, Jesus anticipates the gentile mission that heats up to full steam under the apostle Paul.

JUST WALK AWAY

Here are the clues. The first line in our passage begins with "Jesus left that place," which means not all that much until we read "and went to the vicinity of Tyre" (7:24). The word "region" encompasses a larger area than the port city "Tyre," so we need merely to assume Jesus left the northwest area of Galilee into Phoenicia. Matthew's exact parallel to Mark's verse says Jesus went to the "region of Tyre and Sidon," with the latter city even farther north on the coast of the Mediterranean. Mark 7:26 says she was a "Greek, born in Syrian Phoenicia." It's about forty miles from Capernaum to Tyre, with Sidon another ten miles. We're reading about a minimum of two, but probably three to four, day's journey. Definitely out of sight for the temple agents sent from Jerusalem.

Jesus "left the vicinity of Tyre" and, going the opposite direction of where he ends up in Mark's next passage, that is he went north "through Sidon" and then wended his way back to Galilee but, instead of returning to his previous site of ministry, he skirts by and ends up in "the region of the Decapolis" (7:31). Either Mark did not know the geography or, more likely, he knew Jesus was in no particular hurry to get to the Decapolis.

Jesus needed time to let the heat dissipate and the temple agents to return to Jerusalem. Even more, his strategy to persuade the crowds to embrace him and his kingdom vision needed time away for prayer, for rest, and for teaching his kingdom agents, the apostles. Time away, however, did not do anything but put more needy people on his path. Jesus simply cannot get away from himself.

YOUR GIFTS GO WITH YOU

Near Tyre he enters into a house. He's in a house in a stereotypical enemy territory. Josephus describes how both the Egyptians and the Phoenicians have never had a liking for the Jews. But of the Phoenicians the Tyrians are filled with the most rancor: "while of the Phoenicians it is known the

Tyrians have been most of all in the same ill disposition towards us" (*Against Apion* 1.70).

True to the strategy for his popularity, he "did not want anyone to know it" but, healer that he was, "he could not keep his presence secret" (7:24). A woman—a woman, a gentile, a Phoenician, and a Tyrian—with a daughter who herself had a contaminating spirit (unclean, which means unfit for the temple) bows down to Jesus pleading for her daughter. Jesus' response, by most accounts, is blunt and uses a stereotype. Very common, and today it would be very insensitive.

As Bonnie Bowman Thurston observes: ". . . as we see a sharp-witted Gentile woman, one who is altruistic, persistent and inventive, who does not hesitate to approach Jesus, and a Jesus who learns from a woman, who transcends the racist and sexist boundaries of his culture, who recognizes insights from outside the pale and acknowledges that faith can be found there too." (Thurston, "Mark," 555).

She's a gentile, and Jesus' normal audience is Jewish. Jesus then uses a typical slur for gentiles ("dogs") and says the "children" (Israel) need the food. His words do not put off this mom, so she turns a corner with his script with some "sass" to observe that children often (ours sure did) feed the dogs under the table (7:27–28; I take "sass" from Powery, 136). Mark sets up his audience in using this slur so that they can envision the breadth of Jesus' compassion and kingdom redemption. And, clearly, Jesus sets her up for a clever response. Maybe he said "dogs" with a wink and a nod. And maybe he learned something from this gentile woman! Jesus loves her response. "For such a reply, you may go; the demon has left your daughter" (7:29), and she experienced the reality of the redemption when she got home to find her daughter well.

Now down in the Decapolis "some people" bring to Jesus a disabled man who was "deaf and could hardly talk" (that is, aphasic). Jesus puts his redemptive fingers on the man's ears and on the man's tongue, utters in Aramaic that they be opened, and "At this, the man's ears were opened" and "his tongue was loosened" (7:33–35). With eyes and speech, he is restored to community as the disabled man becomes abled. True to form, and in his strategy to let his popularity die down, he "commanded them not to tell anyone," but "they kept talking" (7:36). His popularity, instead of dying down, expands into gentile territories.

One of our graduates from Northern Seminary is pastor Derwin Gray, of Transformation Church on the border of North and South Carolina. He was a former NFL football player who was also a compulsive stutterer. But when he was redeemed by Jesus and turned his life over to him, Jesus touched his tongue and his stuttering began to disappear, and today he is a preacher of the gospel. Jesus is still touching tongues, with a hat tip to Lauren Daigle.

Jesus tried to dismiss the crowds, to get away, and to calm down his popularity, but wherever he went his kingdom powers went with him. Again, Jesus can't get away from himself. Thank God.

QUESTIONS FOR REFLECTION AND APPLICATION

1. How does this section begin to foreshadow the later gentile mission?

2. What do you think of Jesus' interaction with this mother? Why does he use the language he chooses?

3. Mark notes sometimes that Jesus spoke Aramaic during some of his miracles. What do you think of that?

4. Have you ever had to walk away from a ministry to better follow God? What was that like?

5. How might God be calling you to minister to people outside of traditional ministry or church?

FOR FURTHER READING

Beth Moore, *All My Knotted-Up Life: A Memoir* (Carol Stream: Tyndale Momentum, 2023).

JESUS OF THE CROSS: THE BREAD MAKER

Mark 8:1–10

¹ *During those days another large crowd gathered. Since they had nothing to eat, Jesus called his disciples to him and said,* ² *"I have compassion for these people; they have already been with me three days and have nothing to eat.* ³ *If I send them home hungry, they will collapse on the way, because some of them have come a long distance."*

⁴ *His disciples answered, "But where in this remote place can anyone get enough bread to feed them?"*

⁵ *"How many loaves do you have?" Jesus asked.*

"Seven," they replied.

⁶ *He told the crowd to sit down on the ground. When he had taken the seven loaves and given thanks, he broke them and gave them to his disciples to distribute to the people, and they did so.* ⁷ *They had a few small fish as well; he gave thanks for them also and told the disciples to distribute them.* ⁸ *The people ate and were satisfied. Afterward the disciples picked up seven basketfuls of broken pieces that were left over.* ⁹ *About four thousand were present. After he had sent them away,* ¹⁰ *he got into the boat with his disciples and went to the region of Dalmanutha.**

---

* No one knows where this village was. Matthew changes "Dalmanutha" to

For a human being to become mentored into a mature practice of following Jesus, a wise teacher, clear examples, as well as time, discipline, and failure are necessary. You and I can cluck and chuckle about these boneheaded disciples because they wonder how in the world Jesus could feed so many people. We all know they had already been to this dance and were actually on the floor with Jesus. As indicated already, the disciples are on a journey from no faith or even anti-faith to faith to a deeper pilgrimage into faith. They are in-between when the events in the Gospels are described by Mark. Above all the Gospel writers, Mark is the most critical of the disciples' faith.

In the previous feeding story Mark points to the salient factors: they both had not comprehended the revelation of Jesus' feeding and their hearts were still in a softening phase. They had moved well beyond the crowds, but they were not where they would be in ten or more years. We should then see a spitting image of our own faith development in the disciples more than a group to look down upon. Think about your own phases of discipleship: zeal, flagging zeal, flatness, fired up again, revival, distractions, and on and on. Think about the many today who are "deconstructing" and have become Nones who love Jesus but are not too keen on the church. Faith, like love, is a lifetime experience, not a one-and-done event.

FAITH ELICITS COMPASSION

The word compassion translates an emotion word that describes Jesus seeing a person in need and his internal organs twisting in

---

"Magadan," which could also be "Magdala," a prosperous first century fishing village, home of Mary Magdalene.

pain as he empathizes with the person's pain, which prompts him to act to relieve and heal the person. The Gospel writers frequently describe a Jesus with compassion. Most likely they can describe him this way because they saw tears in his eyes and some other visceral expressions of his feelings.

Compassion in Mark

Jesus was indignant. He reached out his hand and touched the man. "I am willing," he said. "Be clean!" (1:41)

When Jesus landed and saw a large crowd, he had compassion on them, because they were like sheep without a shepherd. So he began teaching them many things. (6:34)

"I have compassion for these people; they have already been with me three days and have nothing to eat." (8:2)

"It has often thrown him into fire or water to kill him. But if you can do anything, take pity on us and help us." (9:22)

It is a "large crowd" again, and it is most likely this occurs in gentile territory; they had "nothing to eat," and they had been with him for three days. This in itself reveals the heart of Jesus' kingdom mission and the reason the temple authorities are concerned about Jesus. The seemingly gentile crowds love him, and they are willing to go with him unprepared for wherever their journey might lead.

The interaction of Jesus and the disciples more or less repeats the previous feeding story's interaction (cf. 6:35–38). Their question, "Where in this remote place can anyone find provisions?" perhaps suggests that they did not think Jesus could do in gentile territory what he had done in a Jewish location (Galilee). This time they've got seven loaves of bread and a "few small fish" (8:5, 7). Jesus gives thanks and distributes them to the disciples who become agents of Jesus' food-making powers by distributing them to the people, and once again the well never drains: "seven basketfuls of broken pieces . . . were left over" (8:8). This time there were 4,000, and as with the previous feeding story, they get into a boat and withdraw from the crowds.

Jesus has now done a feeding miracle for both his Jewish crowds in Galilee and for his gentile crowds in the Decapolis. The crumbs falling from the table (7:28) have turned into basketfuls of provisions. As Emerson Powery reminds us, "Perhaps Jesus' miraculous provisions on *both the Jewish and the Gentile sides* might offer contemporary folk guidance in today's struggle against poverty among all ethnic groups" (Powery, "Mark," 137).

FAITH ELICITS SATISFACTION

I'm captured by "the people ate and were satisfied" (8:8). The term behind the word "satisfied," when used for food eaten, can mean bloated, filled up, full. Combine "satisfied" with seven big baskets and think what that suggests. God's provisions are not only unlimited but even what we drain from his wells of goodness never make a dent in his resources. No, more than even that. There is *more left over than was originally distributed*. Remember, all they had was seven loaves and a few fishes, but the leftover was seven big baskets full of pieces of bread.

Jesus did not give the food to the 4,000. He gave the food to the disciples to give to the crowds of hungry folks. Therein is something for you and for me. Instead of telling others to pray for provisions, we are called to be agents of distribution to those in need, and we distribute on behalf of Jesus as a witness to his kingdom mission and holistic redemption.

We think of food in a zero-sum game. If you eat five chicken nuggets, then the one with you only gets five because there are ten total. If you eat six, your friend gets four. When ten are eaten, the carton is empty. But with God, we eat our share and our fill. Then we look into the carton and there are more left than when we began. I can explain this only one way: God's provisions swell in the giving, and our gratitude grows in the receiving.

On the way to the Cross, the disciples need to grow in their belief that God's resources are both infinite and available to those who trust God. But faith here transcends believing God *can* provide. Faith requires us to go with Jesus, knowing God can and *will* provide. Faith gives us eyes to see those in need, and it elicits our compassion for others. Faith then can raise the hands of witness and thanks that God *has* provided *for us*. Ours is to hold out our hands, as before the Lord's Table, to receive the good gifts from God, and then ours is to open our hands to the needs of others. Tim Gombis has a beautiful expression for this when he says we need to rid ourselves of a zero-sum calculation of limited goods to an "imagination of abundance" (Gombis, *Mark*, 271).

QUESTIONS FOR REFLECTION
AND APPLICATION

1. What factors are necessary for people to mature in discipleship?

2. What is your impression of Mark's critiques of the disciples' faith (or lack thereof) in his Gospel?

3. What do you think of the significance of Jesus doing feeding miracles for both Jews and gentiles?

4. How would you describe your own phases of growth as a disciple of Jesus?

5. In what ways could you serve as an agent of distribution for God's generous provision?

JESUS OF THE CROSS: GROWING VISION

Mark 8:11–26

[11] *The Pharisees came and began to question Jesus. To test him, they asked him for a sign from heaven.* [12] *He sighed deeply and said, "Why does this generation ask for a sign? Truly I tell you, no sign will be given to it."*

[13] *Then he left them, got back into the boat and crossed to the other side.*

[14] *The disciples had forgotten to bring bread, except for one loaf they had with them in the boat.* [15] *"Be careful," Jesus warned them. "Watch out for the yeast of the Pharisees and that of Herod."*

[16] *They discussed this with one another and said, "It is because we have no bread."*

[17] *Aware of their discussion, Jesus asked them: "Why are you talking about having no bread? Do you still not see or understand? Are your hearts hardened?* [18] *Do you have eyes but fail to see, and ears but fail to hear? And don't you remember?* [19] *When I broke the five loaves for the five thousand, how many basketfuls of pieces did you pick up?"*

"Twelve," they replied.

²⁰ *And when I broke the seven loaves for the four thousand, how many basketfuls of pieces did you pick up?"*

They answered, "Seven."

²¹ *He said to them, "Do you still not understand?"*

²² *They came to Bethsaida, and some people brought a blind man and begged Jesus to touch him. ²³ He took the blind man by the hand and led him outside the village. When he had spit on the man's eyes and put his hands on him, Jesus asked, "Do you see anything?"*

²⁴ *He looked up and said, "I see people; they look like trees walking around."*

²⁵ *Once more Jesus put his hands on the man's eyes. Then his eyes were opened, his sight was restored, and he saw everything clearly. ²⁶ Jesus sent him home, saying, "Don't even go into the village."*

Some understand, some don't. What surprises is that those who do are the most unlikely. What is not surprising is that our comprehension of Jesus takes time to sink in, to fertilize our hearts and minds, to begin to work its way into our whole bodies and lives. The early stages of our faith can be swamped with enthusiasms and fresh learnings that we begin to ask ourselves *What's left to learn?* Until we meet a logjam, until something immoral stuns our self-perceptions, until a challenging theological idea overmatches our faith, until . . . There are lots of challenges to the faith, and it takes a lifetime (or longer) to mature into an unshakeable foundation. Those most certain in this lifetime are hiding their fears and suppressing their questions. They've mastered hiding and suppressing, but they have not mastered faith. It takes time, a lifetime.

We've got another sandwich structure in this passage (see the translation above). It's simple, and it's profound at the same time. The Pharisees don't understand Jesus, the disciples don't understand, but a blind man sees. That he sees in two phases suggests that those who do comprehend Jesus have to grow into it. So let's not point long fingers at either the Pharisees or the disciples.

GROANING ABOUT THE PHARISEES

Mark glues a few lines about the Pharisees between feeding 4,000 and some teachings to the disciples in a boat. What he says about the Pharisees is brief: They test Jesus, they question Jesus, and they press him for a "sign" (8:11). These questions are posed to Jesus just after the second feeding miracle, and if there's a sign, those are it! Demanding, following those two events, then seems a sure sign of dull perception. Yet, Jesus says, "no sign will be given to it" and he departs (8:12–13). Jesus groans (NIV: "sighed deeply") about the Pharisees. One has to think Jesus won't do signs to prove himself, and along with that, Jesus believes the truthfulness of who he is can be discerned by those who listen to him, by those who come to know him, and by perceiving his mighty deeds as revelations of God's kingdom redemption through him. Tim Gombis is right: "looking for a sign to judge ultimate realities is a bad idea" (Gombis, *Mark*, 278). Asking for more than what God reveals thumbs one's nose at God.

With this back-and-forth Mark sets the stage for the next passage.

QUESTIONING THE DISCIPLES

That his close followers forgot bread gave Jesus an opportunity to play with a word: "Watch out for the yeast of the Pharisees and that of Herod" (8:14–15). The disciples, as they do so often (see John 4:27–38), get stuck in stupid and wonder if Jesus is not talking about their lack of bread. This

Jesus turns into revealing the inner meaning of the bread miracles and the contaminating influences of the Pharisees and Herodians. Actually, Jesus rebukes the disciples (Mark 8:17–21). In essence, their accurate answers to his questions about how much was leftover after each miracle was all they needed to comprehend the meaning of what he did: The Bread Maker is God's agent of the kingdom.

HEALING A BLIND MAN

Perception of who Jesus is and what Jesus is doing takes time. Which is the point of the healing of the blind man in two stages (8:22–26). Jesus applies spit to a blind man's eyes. He gains sight but his vision is blurred. So Jesus applies his hands and "his eyes were opened" and "he saw everything clearly" (8:25). Jesus, the Bread Maker, is also the Sight Giver.

What was a miracle for the man was a parable for the followers of Jesus. They were on their way to deeper and deeper perception. The path to full perception would prove to crash into their standard perceptions of how God redeems and liberates. If they struggled in coming to terms with the bread miracles, when Jesus reveals that he, as Messiah, will be crucified at the hands of the leaders of Jerusalem will more than crash into expectations. It will shock the disciples into a brand new world, one in which the cross becomes the paradigm of God's love.

QUESTIONS FOR REFLECTION AND APPLICATION

1. Why is it important to express fears and doubts in a journey of faith, rather than hiding and suppressing them?

2. How does Jesus use the bread multiplication to make a metaphorical warning about "yeast"?

3. What might the stages of this healing miracle imply about the slow, gradual pace of our growth in faith?

4. What do you do when you feel frustrated about the pace of growth in your spiritual life?

5. Imagine you could have a conversation with a younger version of yourself. What advice from the future would you give about following Jesus?

Special Note to the Reader: For the reflection on Mark 8:27– 9:1, see pp. 5–6.

JESUS OF THE CROSS: BEYOND THE CROSS, THE GLORY

Mark 9:2–13

2 After six days Jesus took Peter, James and John with him and led them up a high mountain, where they were all alone. There he was transfigured before them. 3 His clothes became dazzling white, whiter than anyone in the world could bleach them. 4 And there appeared before them Elijah and Moses, who were talking with Jesus.

5 Peter said to Jesus, "Rabbi, it is good for us to be here. Let us put up three shelters—one for you, one for Moses and one for Elijah." 6 (He did not know what to say, they were so frightened.)

7 Then a cloud appeared and covered them, and a voice came from the cloud: "This is my Son, whom I love. Listen to him!"

8 Suddenly, when they looked around, they no longer saw anyone with them except Jesus.

9 As they were coming down the mountain, Jesus gave them orders not to tell anyone what they had seen until the Son of Man had risen from the dead. 10 They kept the matter to themselves, discussing what "rising from the dead" meant.

11 And they asked him, "Why do the teachers of the law say that Elijah must come first?"

¹² *Jesus replied, "To be sure, Elijah does come first, and restores all things. Why then is it written that the Son of Man must suffer much and be rejected?* ¹³ *But I tell you, Elijah has come, and they have done to him everything they wished, just as it is written about him."*

When I was in college, I became fascinated with the major events in the life of Jesus. By "major" I meant events like the transfiguration. What I wanted to know was *Why did these events occur? Why was Jesus transfigured? Was he transformed in front of these three disciples for their benefit or for his own benefit?* Both. David deSilva calls this event a "spoiler" of the future resurrection of Jesus (deSilva, *In Season*, 48–56).

FOR HIMSELF

Though our reflection on the passage in Mark previous to today's passage, that is on Mark 8:27–9:1, was discussed earlier in this Bible Study, only the revelation that Jesus predicted to the disciples sets the context for today's passage. In that previous passage Jesus revealed that he, the Messiah, will "suffer many things" by the temple leaders of Jerusalem and that he "must be killed" (8:31; the NIV adds a second "must"). Yes, he declared as well that he would be raised. The transfiguration of Jesus turns "rise again" into an event.

As the divine plan of the Father maps onto why Jesus uses "must," so the Transfiguration reveals the same Fatherly plan and care. On the mountain Jesus' inner glory begins to glow so bright his clothing dazzles. This glorious display reminds Jesus of his glory beyond the grave. As he would face the cross emotionally sorrowful (14:34), or one could say he was surrounded with pain, so his revelation of his future crucifixion would have led him into a consciousness of that future pain. The Transfiguration reminds Jesus that the cross will be overmatched by Easter. As both the Messiah and a fully human man he needed the assurance of life beyond the crucifixion. Perhaps not many even think about this, but I have a hard time not thinking of it.

Plus, two of the Bible's greats come to be with him. Both Elijah and Moses, the major figures of the Prophets and the Law, "were talking with" Jesus (8:4). These two men show there is life beyond death, and their presence comforts Jesus. These two men also met God on a high mountain (Exodus 24:15–18; 1 Kings 19). Their deaths, too, partook in mystery (Deuteronomy 34:5–8; 2 Kings 2:9–12).

FOR THE DISCIPLES

Mark interrupts Jesus' precious moments with Elijah and Moses by shifting his report to Peter who thinks this is just so incredibly cool, so cool in fact he wants to turn the moment into a long retreat with one another. He wants to build some bivouacs. Mark cuts Peter's words off with, "He did not know what to say, they were so frightened" (9:5–6). I love what comes next. The Father interrupts in an encompassing cloud with a voice that tells Peter to knock it off, to stop talking, and to see that the Son is being revealed in all his glory and that Peter needs to just listen to the Son (9:7).

The last word from the moment of Transfiguration is from the Father. Just like that, it was all done. What was not done, though, was that the Son would speak and the Father's command to listen would be the proper response of the disciples. They were told not to tell a soul about what they witnessed, which one more time emphasizes the pressure on Jesus from Rome and the temple authorities. They became puzzled about not only Jesus' prediction of his death but now about what "rising from the dead" meant—and this can surprise Christians because we have such a developed theology about the afterlife. For Jews the resurrection was a general resurrection and not a one-off event for one person. But they were muttering this outside the hearing of Jesus.

What they did ask about was Elijah, and this just can't be noticed without reminding us all of how easy it is to get into the weeds of what will happen in the future while missing the major point: Jesus will be raised and that means they too, because they are with him, will be raised. The common Jewish assumption, based on Malachi 4:5–6, of the future return of Elijah popped up at Mark 6:15. His appearance on the "high mountain" with Moses provokes the disciples to ask if what they just witnessed fulfilled that promise in Malachi. Jesus turns them in circles only to say John the Baptist fulfilled that expectation (Mark 9:13). And he was beheaded. Which takes us right back to Jesus predicting his death, and its implication for the followers of Jesus. They, too, will experience pressure from the authorities because they are associated with Jesus' kingdom mission.

But, and here the Transfiguration becomes assurance for the disciples, as Jesus will be raised, as Jesus revealed the glory to come, the disciples can know that beyond a discipleship of the cross is an eternal discipleship in and of glory. David deSilva says this well: "God gave a few key disciples a bit of a break at this point. They were being asked to swallow a whole lot, and they needed something to help them see that, yes, Jesus' vision for his own Messiahship was heading somewhere glorious" (deSilva, *In Season*, 50).

I sound like Mark when I say, *I doubt they caught it*. Not at the time, they didn't. But Peter never forgot this event. Near the end of his life it is this event he recalls, which just shows how assuring this event had become in his life (2 Peter 1:16–18).

QUESTIONS FOR REFLECTION AND APPLICATION

1. What do you find significant about Elijah and Moses appearing at the transfiguration?

2. What did Peter think of that event?

3. Put yourself in the sandals of Jesus' contemporaries, without a developed theology of heaven and eternal life. What might they have thought about his resurrection language?

4. How might resurrection assurance have encouraged the disciples, even while it confused them?

5. What do you believe about life after death?

FOR FURTHER READING

David deSilva, *In Season and Out: Sermons for the Christian Year* (Bellingham, WA: Lexham, 2019).

JESUS OF THE CROSS: THE FAITH JOURNEY

Mark 9:14–29

14 When they came to the other disciples, they saw a large crowd around them and the teachers of the law arguing with them. 15 As soon as all the people saw Jesus, they were overwhelmed with wonder and ran to greet him.

16 "What are you arguing with them about?" he asked.

17 A man in the crowd answered, "Teacher, I brought you my son, who is possessed by a spirit that has robbed him of speech. 18 Whenever it seizes him, it throws him to the ground. He foams at the mouth, gnashes his teeth and becomes rigid. I asked your disciples to drive out the spirit, but they could not."

19 "You unbelieving generation," Jesus replied, "how long shall I stay with you? How long shall I put up with you? Bring the boy to me."

20 So they brought him. When the spirit saw Jesus, it immediately threw the boy into a convulsion. He fell to the ground and rolled around, foaming at the mouth.

21 Jesus asked the boy's father, "How long has he been like this?"

"From childhood," he answered. 22 "It has often thrown him into fire or water to kill him. But if you can do anything, take pity on us and help us."

²³ " 'If you can'?" said Jesus. "Everything is possible for one who believes."

²⁴ Immediately the boy's father exclaimed, "I do believe; help me overcome my unbelief!"

²⁵ When Jesus saw that a crowd was running to the scene, he rebuked the impure spirit. "You deaf and mute spirit," he said, "I command you, come out of him and never enter him again."

²⁶ The spirit shrieked, convulsed him violently and came out. The boy looked so much like a corpse that many said, "He's dead." ²⁷ But Jesus took him by the hand and lifted him to his feet, and he stood up.

²⁸ After Jesus had gone indoors, his disciples asked him privately, "Why couldn't we drive it out?"

²⁹ He replied, "This kind can come out only by prayer."

We all find the last line of today's passage to be a problem. Does it mean not only that we need to believe beyond wavering faith, that is to grow deeper in our faith, for a miracle to occur? Or does it mean even that if we had enough faith, if we had more faith, we'd get all the miracles we want?

I want to answer these questions, but I know what I have to say is not very satisfying, especially to those who are praying 24-7 for a loved one for something they are passionate about. My answer is *The answer to both questions is No, and that seems to smash right into the very words of Jesus.*

A BRIEF SUMMARY

The other-than-the-Transfiguration-disciples, the very ones connected to Jesus the Water Walker, Bread Maker, Sight Giver, and Demon Exorciser, the ones upon whom Jesus poured out his gifts and ordered them to go do likewise (6:7, 12–13)—those disciples were unable to exorcise a demon from a man's precious son (9:14–18). Their inability led to an argument with the scribes (9:14). Jesus rebukes that "unbelieving generation" (9:19), orders the boy to be brought to him, the spirit in the boy reacts to the presence of Jesus, the father wonders aloud *if* Jesus can do something, and Jesus utters a famous word: "Everything is possible for one who believes" (9:23). The man does believe but thinks he needs more faith, Jesus rebukes the "impure spirit," and the boy is liberated (9:24–27). Then Jesus entered into a house where his disciples ask, "Why couldn't we drive it out?" (9:28). Jesus says, "This kind can come out only by prayer" (9:29).

Two of Jesus's words about prayer or intercession jump out and have inspired many believers but just as much these faith words have deflated and discouraged believers.

1. "Everything is possible for one who believes."
2. "This kind can come out only by prayer."

What to say?

REFLECTIONS

First, Jesus loved to speak in hyperbole and exaggeration. Lots of ancient teachers did. More impact results from "the whole world is falling apart" than "our corner of the world has a major vote to decide." It is a fact that not *everything* is possible. One can't by faith believe God into nonexistence or the sky into green. No believers have gotten everything they wanted.

Second, the specific context surrounding these two sayings clarifies that people are questioning how to exorcise one stubborn demon. One should be wary to turn what Jesus says here about everything and anything we want.

Third, as we have shown, faith develops over time from initial trust to ongoing trust to faithfulness but no one in the pages of the Bible ever gets to pure faith all the time. Only God—Father, Son, Spirit—operate at the level of pure trust in one another.

Fourth, the disciples' faltering journey into a fuller faith corresponds to their previous faith failures. We saw three examples in Mark's eighth chapter: at the second feeding miracle, on the boat when Jesus warned them about the yeast of the Pharisees and Herod, and when Peter flops in front of everyone in rebuking Jesus when Jesus says he, the Messiah, will be killed (and raised). Add to this Peter's moment of misunderstanding at the Transfiguration. Put all this together and the two famous words of Jesus about faith and prayer are to be read as exhortations to his disciples to practice faith more deeply so their faith will mature and be ready for bigger challenges to come, like the Cross.

Faith formation requires practice over time to become mature faith. These nuggets from Lil Copan's wonderful novel, *Little Hours*, say it well:

> And I know that prayer is also the way you bend toward God and others.
>
> The shape of our lives matter most, not in the way we see them, but in how God sees them: their potential, their place.
>
> When you get stuck and lose Jesus, you start cleaning. Work at the things you know. Jesus comes back. That's what I do. You practice faith, until you have faith. We practice all our lives (Copan, *Little Hours*, 82, 211, 244).

If prayer bends us toward God, it bends us as well toward the Jesus of the Cross. We would not be off base thinking Jesus' two words about faith are words that turn our hearts and hands more toward him.

QUESTIONS FOR REFLECTION
AND APPLICATION

1. How have you heard these statements of Jesus interpreted before? "Everything is possible for one who believes" and "This kind can come out only by prayer."

2. Does the explanation in this section satisfy you? Why or why not?

3. How do you relate to the disciples' frustration with Jesus, his instructions, and his mission here?

4. What is something you are praying passionately about but have not yet received an answer?

5. How can you continue to practice faith formation over time, even when it is hard, confusing, or discouraging?

FOR FURTHER READING

Lil Copan, *Little Hours: A Novel* (Falmouth, Mass.:
    One Bird Books, 2021).

JESUS OF THE CROSS: THE CROSS LIFE AGAIN

Mark 9:30–37

³⁰ *They left that place and passed through Galilee. Jesus did not want anyone to know where they were,* ³¹ *because he was teaching his disciples. He said to them, "The Son of Man is going to be delivered into the hands of men. They will kill him, and after three days he will rise."* ³² *But they did not understand what he meant and were afraid to ask him about it.*

³³ *They came to Capernaum. When he was in the house, he asked them, "What were you arguing about on the road?"* ³⁴ *But they kept quiet because on the way they had argued about who was the greatest.*

³⁵ *Sitting down, Jesus called the Twelve and said, "Anyone who wants to be first must be the very last, and the servant of all."*

³⁶ *He took a little child whom he placed among them. Taking the child in his arms, he said to them,* ³⁷ *"Whoever welcomes one of these little children in my name welcomes me; and whoever welcomes me does not welcome me but the one who sent me."*

In Mark's Gospel Jesus predicts his death three times (8:31–33; 9:30–32; 10:32–34). Each of those passion predictions leads into Jesus teaching about the cross life for the disciples

(8:34–9:1; 9:33–37; 10:35–45). Their connections did not just happen. The life of Jesus shapes the life of a disciple because the essence of discipleship is following Jesus in trust and allegiance. The Christian life and the cross deserve deeper connections, especially if we tend to emphasize joy and victory and the greatness of church glory. As Dietrich Bonhoeffer once put it, "The call to be extraordinary is the great, inevitable danger of discipleship" (*Discipleship*, 148).

PREDICTION

One more time Jesus seeks invisibility to the Roman and Jerusalem powers, and this time Mark tells us he did so in order to find time to mentor his disciples (9:30–31). Part of his mentoring was to prepare them for his death at the "hands of men." One more time, in their continual journey of faith, "they did not understand and were afraid to ask him about it" (9:32).

INSTRUCTION

When they all got to Capernaum Jesus queried the disciples about their argument on the path. They sheepishly, perhaps, admitted that they were yacking about who was the greatest of the disciples (9:33–34). From their fear of asking him about the prediction of death to their being quiet about their rivalries we learn where these disciples are in the faith journey: *not far enough yet!*

So Jesus, "sitting down," utters a word more piercing than those faith words in the previous passage: "Anyone who wants to be first must be the very last, and the servant of all" (9:35). This verse anticipates a fuller discussion of the very same theme in 10:35–45, but for now we are right back with Mark's thematic passage, Mark 8:27–9:1. If Jesus is the

Messiah of the Cross, and their calling is to follow him, then discipleship is a discipleship of the Cross. Which means not driving for glory and honor and fame and the extraordinary. It means being a "servant" (our word is "deacon") of "all" (9:35).

All gets real when he puts a child in the middle of the circle and says, Look, reception of a child as a follower of mine is a reception of me—rejection of a child is a rejection of me (9:37). Children in those days and in our days easily become invisible. Just ask anyone who ministers to children. Here is a word from a Dead Sea Scroll, and I have put in bold the words to fasten your eyes upon:

> Everything that is revealed from the Law for the multitude of the Camp, and in which he (the postulant) has imperfect knowledge, the Overseer should tell him and command him to study for one full year; and then according to his knowledge he may draw near. But no one who is a fool or insane may enter; and no simpleton or ignoramus or one with eyes too weak to see or lame or crippled or deaf **or minor child**, none of these shall enter the congregation, for the holy angels are in your midst (Damascus Document [=CD] 15:13–17).

Instructions like this occur a number of times in the Dead Seas Scrolls, one time mentioning a youth, but what stands out here is with whom a child is classified. Not just the ignored and invisible but those deemed unworthy of proximity to God.

Jesus knows what he is doing when placing a child in their midst. Jesus makes "all" visible in this moment with a child representing all the unworthies. He hereby reminds them that the calling of a follower of Jesus is to serve those on the path or in our way according to their needs. Serving any and all is a cross life for Jesus. Again, Bonhoeffer: "But how should disciples know what their cross is? They will receive it when they begin to follow the suffering Lord. They will recognize their cross in communion with Jesus" (Bonhoeffer, *Discipleship*, 89). As we follow along with Jesus our faith becomes more and more like the Jesus of the Cross because his presence influences who we are.

QUESTIONS FOR REFLECTION AND APPLICATION

1. What is the essence of discipleship?

2. How did Jesus balance the needs of the crowds for his healing and the needs of his disciples for his presence?

3. What does Jesus mean when he holds up a child as an example of faith and faithfulness?

4. Who are people considered "unworthies" in your community?

5. What was your experience of faith community as a child? Did you ever feel welcome and important?

FOR FURTHER READING

Dietrich Bonhoeffer, *Discipleship* (Dietrich Bonhoeffer Works; Minneapolis: Fortress, 2011). Formerly called *The Cost of Discipleship*.

JESUS OF THE CROSS: REWARDS FOR DISCIPLES

Mark 9:38–50

1

[38] *"Teacher," said John, "we saw someone driving out demons **in your name** and we told him to stop, because he was not one of us."*

[39] *"Do not stop him," Jesus said. "For no one who does a miracle **in my name** can in the next moment say anything bad about me,* [40] *for whoever is not against us is for us.*

2

[41] *Truly I tell you, anyone who gives you a cup of water **in my name** because you belong to the Messiah will certainly not lose their reward.*

3

[42] *"If anyone causes one of these little ones—those who believe in me—to stumble, it would be better for them if a large millstone were hung around their neck and they were thrown into the sea.* [43] *If your hand causes you to stumble, cut it off. It is better for you to enter life maimed than with two hands to go into hell, where the*

fire never goes out. *⁴⁵ And if your foot causes you to stumble, cut it off. It is better for you to enter life crippled than to have two feet and be thrown into hell. ⁴⁷ And if your eye causes you to stumble, pluck it out. It is better for you to enter the kingdom of God with one eye than to have two eyes and be thrown into hell, ⁴⁸ where*

> " 'the worms that eat them do not die,
>   and the **fire** is not quenched.'

4
*⁴⁹ Everyone will be **salted** with **fire**.*

5
*⁵⁰ "**Salt** is good, but if it loses its saltiness, how can you make it salty again? Have salt among yourselves, and be at peace with each other."*

Today's passage can be separated into five units, and the first and second are tied together (in bold letters) by "in your name" and the fourth and fifth by "fire" and "salt." The middle unit helps to clarify the theme for all five: the reward for those who follow Jesus. Jesus, like his contemporaries, used the word "reward" often though it appears only at 9:41 in the Gospel of Mark. (The term will be discussed more in the Everyday Bible Study on Matthew at Matthew 5:12.) Reward language compels a person to think of one's eternal destiny, which is why Jesus uses reward language.

Some followers of Jesus today become edgy about what happens after death or what will occur in the world in the end times. Some deny the importance of thinking about heaven or the kingdom of God. Instead, they believe we should only talk and think about the here and now. One cannot read Jesus and come away with anything but a view of life where *now* matters so much because *the future* matters even more. Yes, those on the edge have good reasons to bellyache about too many parents and preachers who resort to hell all the time or who diminish the importance of life *now*. But the present for Jesus matters so much because he knows the future is eternal. Today's passage makes no sense until one embraces a now that matters because the future matters more.

Security about the future ought not, however, breed pride about one's group, as if one's group is the only group faithful to Jesus. The answer to the old hymn about who is on the Lord's side will surprise everyone! Only God knows. Groupy-ness has got to go from the church.

FOR US AND AGAINST US

Exorcisms abounded in the ancient world, some of them connected to magic and others straight from the Spirit of God (Matthew 12:28). One of Jesus' inner mission agents, John son of Zebedee, perhaps one arguing about greatness (Mark 9:34), informs Jesus of an exorcist doing his powers in the "name" of Jesus, to which Jesus replies with two stunningly generous, even expansive and inclusive, statements.

> Statement #1: "For no one who does a miracle in my name can in the next moment say anything bad about me" (9:39).
> Statement #2: "for whoever is not against us is for us" (9:40).

Jesus contends that anyone who does a work of power, and the word indicates liberating someone from the Devil's grip, in his name is on Jesus' team. The use of "in my name" means the power at work does not derive from the exorcist himself or herself, nor does it work because of some ritual magical formula said, nor does it come from some superstitious objects.

It was common enough for exorcists to have a bowl of water and a ring. Go figure. Jesus affirms anyone who knows the power of God is connected to Jesus. If the exorcist is both affirming Jesus' power and not discrediting Jesus (see 3:22), the person is "for us" (9:40). What matters most then is one's relationship to Jesus.

REWARD, IN OTHER WORDS

Sayings #2 and #3 express eternal life with various expressions. The first one (9:41) expresses the future as a "reward," even though it is said indirectly with "will not lose their reward." It is given to the one who "gives you [disciples of Jesus] a cup of water in my name." As the exorcist is "for us" so the one who gives cold water to a parched person is also "for us." The expansive generosity troubles many who want to think of the people of God in narrow numbers. God loves all, we begin there.

Causing a "little one," and I think of the children in Mark 9:36–37, to be tripped up, fallen down, and collapsed—imagery for losing one's way and not believing and not following Jesus—will, instead of having a reward will have a "large millstone" around the neck and tossed into a sea. A rather graphic image for divine judgment because judgment is the flipside of reward. If language or reward grabs a person's attention about the future, the reverse does too. Jesus shifts the language from millstone to "Gehenna," a historic valley south of Jerusalem where divine judgment occurred/occurs—and this for sins with the hand, foot, and eye (9:43–47).

The future in this short set of verses (#2, #3) comes to expression with these terms: reward, life, and kingdom of God. What leads to that final state are these practices: giving a cup of cold water to a Jesus associate, not causing children to stumble, and hand and foot and eye righteousness. The implication is rather clear: *what we do now and how we live, all in relationship with Jesus, determines our future before God*. Yet, this bold truth is not designed to promote fear. Rather, for the disciples it was assuring. Knowing their walk with Jesus led to the kingdom was another way of saying resurrection and Transfiguration, that is, that beyond the Cross life will be eternal life in the kingdom.

SALT AND FIRE

Drawing on the word "fire" from what Jesus said about Gehenna (9:47–48), Jesus turns into a play on the term "salt." To be salted with fire most likely suggests opposition, persecution, and suffering in the Cross life. The disciplines of controlling one's hand, foot, and eye are the salt of Cross life discipleship while losing control makes the salt insipid and useless. The final line of today's passage surprises most readers because salt there means living in peace with one another (9:49–50). Peace among the disciples turns us around to return to 9:33–34 where the disciples were barking up the wrong tree, the tree of wanting to be great and extraordinary.

QUESTIONS FOR REFLECTION AND APPLICATION

1. What is the reward for those who follow Jesus?

2. Why does the present matter for Jesus?

3. How might we apply warnings about "not causing little ones to stumble" in the church today?

4. Where do you see "groupy-ness" in your faith community?

5. If Christians embraced the philosophy that "whoever is not against us is for us," how might that impact unity in the church?

JESUS OF THE CROSS: MARRIAGE AND DIVORCE

Mark 10:1–12

[1] *Jesus then left that place and went into the region of Judea and across the Jordan. Again crowds of people came to him, and as was his custom, he taught them.*

[2] *Some Pharisees came and tested him by asking, "Is it lawful for a man to divorce his wife?"*

[3] *"What did Moses command you?" he replied.*

[4] *They said, "Moses permitted a man to write a certificate of divorce and send her away."*

[5] *"It was because your hearts were hard that Moses wrote you this law," Jesus replied.* [6] *"But at the beginning of creation God 'made them male and female.'* [7] *'For this reason a man will leave his father and mother and be united to his wife,* [8] *and the two will become one flesh.' So they are no longer two, but one flesh.* [9] *Therefore what God has joined together, let no one separate."*

[10] *When they were in the house again, the disciples asked Jesus about this.* [11] *He answered, "Anyone who divorces his wife and marries another woman commits adultery against her.* [12] *And if she divorces her husband and marries another man, she commits adultery."*

F ew subjects are as sensitive as marriage, divorce, and remarriage; few topics are as pastorally difficult as preaching
about the divorce texts of Jesus. After all, what Jesus teaches
goes. Noticeably, the same sensitivity and difficulty of our day
is nearly matched by the same tensions in the world of Jesus.
So significant was a teacher's view of divorce and remarriage
that Jesus' common challengers, the Pharisees, get Jesus to
state where he stands on the current theological controversy.

As part of his strategy of staying clear of the temple
authorities' watchful eyes, Jesus leaves Galilee and enters
into the "region of Judea and across the Jordan." Try as he may
to escape, the "crowds" find him no matter where he goes.
The good news is that Jesus' vision of the kingdom is so compelling crowds love him, and the bad news is that the crowds
love him. Pharisees, even more popular than Jesus with the
masses, put a question to him as a way of measuring how safe
he was for the temple authorities. One can assume, too, that
Jesus' answer could be used by the Pharisees to garner more
support with the populace.

THE QUESTION

Some questions are designed to draw out of a person an
answer that reveals one's allegiances. Like asking for whom
one voted. Like asking what one thinks of N.T. Wright or
John Piper or Kristin Kobes DuMez. The Pharisees ask about
divorce, not because they have some pastoral concerns and
need Jesus' advice. The Gospels just don't give us the impression the Pharisees and Jesus were friends. At the time of Jesus,
permissions to divorce fell into camps: some were permissive,
some were restrictive. One famous rabbi's statement was that
one could divorce one's wife for trivial kitchen goofups, like

ruining one's dinner. The Pharisees stood tall in the permissive camp. Here is a later statement about two first century rabbis, Shammai (conservative) and Hillel (progressive), that illustrates the context of the question Jesus is asked:

a. The House of Shammai say, "A man should divorce his wife only because he has found grounds for it in unchastity,

b. "since it is said, Because he has found in her indecency in anything (Dt. 24:1)."

c. And the House of Hillel say, "Even if she spoiled his dish,

d. "since it is said, Because he has found in her indecency in anything."

e. R. Aqiba says, "Even if he found someone else prettier than she,

f. "since it is said, And it shall be if she find no favor in his eyes (Dt. 24:1)." (*Mishnah Gittin* 9:10).

Testing him, they ask if it is "permissible." In that world, permissible meant "law-observant." In the evangelical world it means "biblical." They want to know where Jesus stands. If he sides with them, the Pharisees permissiveness is affirmed; if he's against them, they can take it to the temple authorities or to their crowds of followers.

SOME GIVE-AND-TAKE

Jesus's answer begins with the Bible, with a "What did Moses command you?" One of the famous slogans in the Evangelical Covenant Church stands here with Jesus. The slogan is "Where is it written?" The Pharisees immediately answer with a *He says it's OK to divorce* and to do so *to give the woman a "bill of divorce,"* which had a clause that permitted the woman to remarry as a "free" woman, and then *to break off relations with her* (10:3–4).

A Writ of Divorce

R. Judah says, "[In Aramaic]: Let this be from me your writ of divorce, letter of dismissal, and deed of liberation, that you may marry anyone you want."

    a. The text of a writ of emancipation [is as follows]:

    b. "Lo, you are a free girl, lo, you are your own [possession]" [cf. Dt. 21:14] (*Mishnah Gittin* 9:3).

Jesus responds not with *Well done*, but with a surprising answer. He states unequivocally that Moses' command was only granted as a concession to their sinful ways. In fact, Mark uses a strong expression from the Old Testament. God permitted divorce "because your hearts were hard" (10:5; see Jeremiah 4:4). He pushes back to the Creation story of Genesis 1–2 to argue with the Pharisees, who surely enjoyed this discussion about law. There Jesus discovers that God made the two into one flesh, and that "what God has joined together, let no one separate" (Mark 10:9).

Wow! The entire social fabric of the world of Jerusalem discussed legitimate grounds for divorce but not the *legitimacy of divorce or not*. Notice this: *here Jesus is more conservative, far more conservative in fact, than the Pharisees*. Here Jesus stands with the most conservative circles in Jerusalem. He does so on the basis of how he reads the Bible. For Jesus, *divorce is contrary to the design and actions of God.*

THE CLARIFICATION

The closest followers of Jesus, overhearing Jesus' potent stance, gasped. So Jesus clarified what he meant, which only made them gasp some more:

> Anyone who divorces his wife and marries another woman commits adultery against her. And if she divorces her husband and marries another man, she commits adultery (10:11–12).

A plain reading of this text makes two things clear: Jesus is against divorce, and he's against remarriage.

We do know that Matthew's rendering of this event, both in the exact parallel (Matthew 19:3–12) and in a paragraph in the Sermon on the Mount (5:31–32), as well as Luke 16:18, seem not to be so rigid as what Mark has in today's passage. How to explain the differences?

Jesus in Mark trades in a strong statement, probably even exaggerated, because his intent veers from nuance about careful distinctions of what's permissible and what's not. Jesus comprehends the question of the Pharisees as one that assumes generous justifications for divorce. Their more permissive approach deserves a strong counter defense of the inviolability of the marriage covenant and the importance of preserving it at all costs. So, Jesus appeals to Genesis in a way that turns Moses' law in Deuteronomy 24:1–4 into a divine concession, not a law-forming opportunity to find reasons for a divorce.

But, both Matthew and Luke will show that Jesus was not contending Deuteronomy 24 was wrong. There are reasons for divorce, like sexual immorality (Matthew 5:31–32), and the apostle Paul will add yet another in 1 Corinthians 7:10–16. But in Mark's context Jesus is not discussing legitimate grounds for divorce but the importance of marriage in a context where divorce was too permissive.

TODAY

We cannot here enter into a lengthy discussion about divorce and remarriage. And, because Matthew has more than we find in Mark, our discussion will be longer at Matthew 5:31–32. Instead, I'd like to respect Mark for what Mark does, and start where Mark started: with widespread permissibility for divorce, widespread remarriage, and a devaluation of the marriage covenant in the Jewish world. Jesus (in today's passage from Mark) clearly emphasizes the importance of the covenant of marriage and he presses against easy permissions for divorce. Matthew's Gospel will provide exceptions, not because Matthew disagrees with Jesus, but because he knows that Jesus' emphasis pushed against easy permissions. Some in his day were flippant about the marriage covenant and wanted to divorce for any old reason they could find. Mark's presentation emphasizes Jesus' valuation of marriage. That deserves emphasis today.

Our society is far more permissive than the world of Jesus, and modern evangelical Christians are more permissive than what we find in the Gospels and even in 1 Corinthians 7. The church needs more teaching on love, clearer catechisms on the meaning of marriage's commitments, on the safety of expressing marriage problems, and the church will need to work hard on creating environments that nurture reconciliation when it is possible and desired. And it is not always possible, it is not always desired, and sometimes pressing for reconciliation can endanger women and children. While the

Christian fellowship is designed by God to be the pastoral and personal context for individuals pondering divorce (or reconciliation), not all churches and not all leaders in churches are sufficiently safe for those considering divorce, even when it is entirely legitimate. Some church leaders are masculinist powermongers who believe women should submit even to their abusive husbands. Such church contexts are neither safe nor consistent with Jesus. So, while it is wise to consider the church context, it is not always wise. What is wise is to find a safe place for any discussions about marriage and divorce.

Mark does not enter into the space of permissibilities. Instead, Mark's Gospel recounts half the story of what Jesus teaches, a half that some in our churches today need to hear. Namely, that God designs marriage to be life-long. The other half of the story, which deals with the grounds for divorce as well as the harm that some partners in marriage inflict, is not told in Mark. Matthew's Gospel opens that discussion. In essence, Jesus' emphasis on the marriage covenant does not deny the permissibility of divorce in the case of sexual immorality, and Paul's addition of another exception (abandonment because of a partner's Christian faith) sets the tone for Christian wisdom to explore legitimate reasons for divorce. Such permission is clear in Matthew 5:31–32 and in 19:1–12 and 1 Corinthians 7:12–16.

Furthermore, the grounds for divorce stated by Jesus in Matthew 5:31–32 and expanded by Paul in 1 Corinthians 7:12–16 suggest that Christian thinkers, under the guidance of the Spirit and with careful attention to scriptures, have discerned other permissible grounds for divorce. One thinks today of spousal abuse—sexual, physical, psychological, emotional—and child abuse, as well as the kinds of infidelity chosen by some through the internet, dating apps, social media and internet "relationships"—that is, to sexual addictions generated outside of actual physical relationships. The Bible never set out a passage that explicitly stated the only grounds for divorce—these and no more—and so we are called at times to discern permissibility. Permissible grounds lead to permissible divorces. Permissible divorces need to be embraced with love and compassion and fellowship by churches and church leaders. To rewound the already-wounded is unacceptable behavior on the part of church leaders and churches. Even more, permissible divorces can and often do generate a permissible remarriage, and experience shows many new couples flourish in their marriages.

Questions for Reflection and Application

1. What is the Pharisees' strategy to trap Jesus here?

2. How does Jesus handle their challenge?

3. In what ways does Jesus appeal to Scripture that shocks his hearers?

4. How does Mark handle this story about Jesus differently from other Gospel writers?

5. In what ways has divorce impacted your life? How can Jesus' teaching bring healing to you?

JESUS OF THE CROSS: FRESH DISCIPLESHIP IMAGES

Mark 10:13–31

¹³ *People were bringing little children to Jesus for him to place his hands on them, but the disciples rebuked them.* ¹⁴ *When Jesus saw this, he was indignant. He said to them, "Let the little children come to me, and do not hinder them, for the kingdom of God belongs to such as these.* ¹⁵ *Truly I tell you, anyone who will not receive the kingdom of God like a little child will never enter it."* ¹⁶ *And he took the children in his arms, placed his hands on them and blessed them.*

¹⁷ *As Jesus started on his way, a man ran up to him and fell on his knees before him. "Good teacher," he asked, "what must I do to inherit eternal life?"*

¹⁸ *"Why do you call me good?" Jesus answered. "No one is good—except God alone.* ¹⁹ *You know the commandments: 'You shall not murder, you shall not commit adultery, you shall not steal, you shall not give false testimony, you shall not defraud, honor your father and mother.'"*

²⁰ *"Teacher," he declared, "all these I have kept since I was a boy."*

²¹ *Jesus looked at him and loved him. "One thing you lack," he*

said. "Go, sell everything you have and give to the poor, and you will have treasure in heaven. Then come, follow me."

²² At this the man's face fell. He went away sad, because he had great wealth.

²³ Jesus looked around and said to his disciples, "How hard it is for the rich to enter the kingdom of God!"

²⁴ The disciples were amazed at his words. But Jesus said again, "Children, how hard it is to enter the kingdom of God! ²⁵ It is easier for a camel to go through the eye of a needle than for someone who is rich to enter the kingdom of God."

²⁶ The disciples were even more amazed, and said to each other, "Who then can be saved?"

²⁷ Jesus looked at them and said, "With man this is impossible, but not with God; all things are possible with God."

²⁸ Then Peter spoke up, "We have left everything to follow you!"

²⁹ "Truly I tell you," Jesus replied, "no one who has left home or brothers or sisters or mother or father or children or fields for me and the gospel ³⁰ will fail to receive a hundred times as much in this present age: homes, brothers, sisters, mothers, children and fields— along with persecutions—and in the age to come eternal life. ³¹ But many who are first will be last, and the last first."

One can make a long list of the various terms, images, or ideas chosen to express what the Christian life is all about. In my life I have been taught and captured by a variety of images, including separation from the world and holiness, obedience, evangelistic zeal, daily devotions and Bible study, growing in grace, discipleship, gifts of the Spirit, life in the Spirit, social justice, eucharistic worship, love, wisdom, and peace. Each of these expressions empowers followers of Jesus at various times, and each tends to grow dog-eared over time. Since someone seems to be able to summarize her whole life around one term with such a sterling witness to Christ, one can be drawn into the orbit of such a person. But most of us need most of these terms, and more, most of the time. In fact, that's why we find Jesus himself using a variety of expressions to give the way of the Cross fresh expression.

Jesus walks on his fateful path to Jerusalem along with the disciples, teaching them all the way. What occurs in Jerusalem will forever shape the life of Jesus and therefore the way of discipleship. To be attached to Jesus, as the disciples are on this trip to Jerusalem, takes on an entirely new shape when Jesus is arrested, tried, and crucified. During the fateful trip Jesus instructs his disciples with a variety of images. None of these images is the one-and-only image for following Jesus; each is anchored explicitly into a specific moment; and each can offer to us further instruction on what it means to follow the Jesus of the Cross.

DISCIPLES ARE RECEIVERS

A charismatic presence like that of Jesus' drew crowds. Parents wanted their children to observe hope for Judea by bringing them to Jesus. The disciples, once again rather obtuse to the ways of Jesus and annoyed by the presence of these children—are not far from Qumran when this event occurs (see previous text at 9:36–37 for a Dead Sea Scroll text about devaluing children)—encounter not only a stiff rebuke from Jesus for their lack of empathy and compassion, but also a fresh image for what it means to be with Jesus. In saying "stiff rebuke" I am understating what Mark wrote in 10:14. Jesus was angry, and anger can be perceived via body movements, tone, and vocabulary even if they don't say *I'm miffed*.

It's all wrapped up in a simple statement, make that two: "for the kingdom of God belongs to such as these" and "anyone who will not receive the kingdom of God like a little child will never enter it" (10:14, 15). The first makes it clear that, in God's view and unlike the disciples' view, children are part of the kingdom. The second that the unquestioned, trusting reception routinely observed in children forms into a fresh image for discipleship. A disciple is one who trustingly receives the blessing of Jesus (10:16). We often say, "it is better to give than to receive," but many of us need to learn "it is harder to receive than to give." To receive means we are needy, we can't fix it on our own, and what Jesus has is what we need—so we hold out open hands and accept the blessing-gifts of Jesus.

DISCIPLES ARE GIVERS

A dialogue with a wealthy man (Luke makes him a rich ruler; Luke 18:18) moves from a reasonable question, "What must I do to inherit eternal life?" to a puzzling response from Jesus ("Why do you call me good?") attached to a blunt, "No one is good—except God alone" (10:17–18). Those striking responses to the rich man's question are followed up with a list of some of the commands in the Decalogue, which is met with the man's claim that he has always done the commands. Jesus shows no offense by the man's claim. Instead, Jesus ramps up the demand from a Torah observant life to *selling everything he's got, giving the proceeds to the poor,* and then following Jesus (10:19–21). The rich man's "face fell," and he rejected the discipleship demand of Jesus (10:22). Like the seed sown among thorns, the man's wealth choked out sun-bringing-life.

How do you measure who is wealthy? Most of us, and that's a deliberate understatement, measure our wealth by comparing ourselves with others. In the suburbs in which I live that means I can compare our home and income with the obviousness of some massive homes and my guesstimates of their income. But comparing ourselves to others ruins the passage. The question is *What is my record of giving to the poor and using my wealth for the good of others?* Instead of justifying ourselves, we are to hear a challenge from Jesus. Another question we can ask is *What percentage of our church's intake becomes gifts for the poor?*

Jesus clearly did not expect all disciples to give up everything they owned. He dined in the homes of others, and he did not require Peter to leave his home. So, the fresh image that says "sell everything you have" is another example of hyperbole in order to communicate the depth of commitment needed for the rich man. Disciples learn from this encounter that following Jesus requires giving to the poor, and sometimes it means giving up what we have in our present life so we can go where Jesus wants us to go.

DISCIPLES ARE CAMEL-LIKE

Jesus' closest followers, who by now have heard more than their share of shocking teachings by Jesus, were "amazed" when Jesus said it was very difficult for those with an accumulation of possessions "to enter the kingdom of God" (10:23). So Jesus gives an image, and it is yet another example of exaggeration: as a camel can never be threaded through the eye of a needle, so a rich man can't be squeezed into the kingdom. Overstatement, to be sure, but the disciples snagged the force of his saying in their hearts and consciences. Jesus sums up conversions to discipleship of the Cross as "impossible" but an impossibility that God makes possible (10:27).

Perhaps you wonder if what you have heard about camels having to be stripped of their baggage and saddle to crawl through a gate at the entrance to Jerusalem. It's clever but I know of no evidence of such a custom (other than in sermons!). Morna Hooker turns it all around with these words:

> It is only the extraordinary inability of commentators to appreciate the hyperbole and humour in the illustration

179

that has led them to suggest that the camel should be reduced in size to a rope [the Greek word for rope is *kamilos*], or that the **eye of a needle** should be enlarged to an imaginary gate in the wall of Jerusalem. Jesus wished to make his hearers think by presenting them with an absurd picture of the largest animal attempting to go through the tiniest aperture (Hooker, *Mark*, 242–243).

It's wise, then, to avoid literal readings and instead to appreciate the clever grotesqueness.

DISCIPLES ARE SURRENDERERS AND RECEIVERS

To open today's passage we met the image of the importance or receiving and then we turned to the image of giving, and both of those show up in 10:28–31. Peter opines that "we [disciples] have left everything," with emphasis on the word *have*—so what's in it for us? Jesus overlays what they have surrendered "for me and the gospel" with what they will receive. Here's how the package works:

Jesus wants his followers to see that (1) at some level nothing will be lost and (2) that they will discover more than adequate compensation in the family of Jesus. The absence of "father" in the Will Receive column finds compensation in God the Father. One observes a harshness in these two lists. Losing one's family and fields, to be sure, finds a new freshness in the family of Jesus, but one must also recognize the pain involved in the losses–which is at least part of "with persecutions." Plus, Jesus' stronger words on family separations derive both from his own experience (cf. John 7:5) as well as those of his followers who experienced rejection for following him. Jesus is not heartless; he knows from experience the reality of what it costs to follow him.

Surrendered	Will Receive "a hundredfold times as much in this present age . . ."
Home	Homes
Brothers	Brothers
Sisters	Sisters
Mother	Mothers
Father	
Children	Children
Fields	Fields
	"with persecutions
	and in the coming age, eternal life."

He also knows the sweetness of fellowship in the kingdom, of the love between brothers and sisters on the way with him, and of the hope of the kingdom. Those different images for different people at different times. But at the same time different images for each of us as well.

QUESTIONS FOR REFLECTION AND APPLICATION

1. How does Jesus use creative imagery to instruct his disciples?

2. Jesus appears to be angry with the disciples when he gives a "stiff rebuke." List as many words as you can for various types of anger (irritated, furious, etc.). How do you perceive when someone is angry, and how do you identify anger in yourself?

3. How might wealth impact our ability to be faithful followers?

4. What is the hope Jesus offers his disciples in return for the challenges of following him?

5. Of the expressions Jesus uses to explain the way of the Cross, which resonates most with you?

JESUS OF THE CROSS: JUST LIKE JESUS

Mark 10:32–45

³² *They were on their way up to Jerusalem, with Jesus leading the way, and the disciples were astonished, while those who followed were afraid. Again he took the Twelve aside and told them what was going to happen to him.* ³³ *"We are going up to Jerusalem," he said, "and the Son of Man will be delivered over to the chief priests and the teachers of the law. They will condemn him to death and will hand him over to the Gentiles,* ³⁴ *who will mock him and spit on him, flog him and kill him. Three days later he will rise."*

³⁵ *Then James and John, the sons of Zebedee, came to him. "Teacher," they said, "we want you to do for us whatever we ask."*

³⁶ *"What do you want me to do for you?" he asked.*

³⁷ *They replied, "Let one of us sit at your right and the other at your left in your glory."*

³⁸ *"You don't know what you are asking," Jesus said. "Can you drink the cup I drink or be baptized with the baptism I am baptized with?"*

³⁹ *"We can," they answered.*

Jesus said to them, "You will drink the cup I drink and be baptized with the baptism I am baptized with, ⁴⁰ *but to sit at my right or left is not for me to grant. These places belong to those for whom they have been prepared."*

⁴¹ When the ten heard about this, they became indignant with James and John. ⁴² Jesus called them together and said, "You know that those who are regarded as rulers of the Gentiles lord it over them, and their high officials exercise authority over them. ⁴³ Not so with you. Instead, whoever wants to become great among you must be your servant, ⁴⁴ and whoever wants to be first must be slave of all. ⁴⁵ For even the Son of Man did not come to be served, but to serve, and to give his life as a ransom for many."

In the ancient world, education was about emulation more than information, and when it comes to the relationship of a follower of Jesus to Jesus, the "education" was about formation, and the formation Jesus taught was about imitation. Not imitation in a literal manner, but still, discipleship to Jesus means to be conformed to him. If Jesus walks the way of the Cross, disciples do as well. One can't follow Jesus to the Cross and pursue greatness and glory. At least, if one does, one will no longer be following Jesus. Instead, that person will be pursuing his own glory.

Following Jesus, both physically step-by-step and metaphorically as a disciple, the Cross becomes more and more visible to the reader of Mark's Gospel.

PREDICTING THE CROSS

Mark's narrative intentionally creates drama in four short clauses: "They were on their way up to Jerusalem, with Jesus leading the way, and the disciples were astonished, while those who followed were afraid" (10:32). Perhaps his followers are unaware of what will happen in Jerusalem, but we know, and the close reader of Mark knows (8:31; 9:31). In Jerusalem he will meet his divinely destined death. He does not back down, he does not withdraw, and he does not delay: "with Jesus leading the way."

Oddly, some are "astonished," but we are not sure why. The NIV has added "the disciples were astonished" here even though the Greek text does not have that term. The NIV does this because a contrast occurs: some were astonished *but the ones following were afraid* (10:32). The two emotions are not the same, but they could be related. Perhaps Mark's grammar can be explained as merely inelegant, and the two emotions are coming from the same group, namely the disciples. After all, the word "those who *followed*" most likely refers to disciples. Disciples, too, have shown fear before in this Gospel. Now realizing that Jesus has already predicted his death twice, now getting closer and closer to the City, his followers become fearful over what awaits Jesus and, therefore, what awaits them. Mark's theme is all here: the Jesus of the Cross calls his followers to a discipleship of the Cross.

On the trip to Jerusalem, and they have not yet reached Jericho (10:46), Jesus predicts a third time that he will be killed in Jerusalem (8:31; 9:31; 10:33–34). The fate will be engineered by temple authorities in Jerusalem. Notice the absence of the Pharisees; the moves will be made by one who gives him over to "the chief priests [Caiaphas, Annas] and teachers of the law" (10:33) who, in turn, will hand him over to the "Gentiles," namely, the Roman authorities (Pilate, Antipas). One can assume the disciples, astonished and fearful as they were, did not grip on to "three days later he will rise" (10:34).

Jesus will not shake himself free from the Cross.

CHALLENGING THE CROSS

The next section of today's passage, were it not so disappointing, would be comedy. Two brothers, two of his closest followers, probably two relatives—"James and John"—ask an ambiguous question, and Jesus requests clarity. They give it with "Let one of us sit at your right and the other at your left in your glory" (10:37). Maybe the disciples did snag Jesus' word predicting his resurrection. Maybe these two brothers have jumped all the way from this ascent into Jerusalem into the final kingdom of God. What they have jumped to is glory and status and honor, and they can make that jump only because of ambition, if not arrogance. The two consider themselves dual MVPs of the apostles. They want to be celebrities.

They have challenged, just like Peter, the legitimacy and at least the reality of the Cross, something toward which Jesus was ascending. They want glory by skipping the nightmare of the last days of Jesus. They want Easter without Maundy Thursday or Good Friday. They want a kingdom banquet without the last supper.

So Jesus pushes back on their challenge, first by telling them they're clueless and then by asking questions hinged to metaphors: "Can you drink the cup I drink or be baptized with the baptism I am baptized with?" (10:38). Their glory dreams jump over the Cross again with "We can" (10:39). Jesus momentarily plays out their affirmations while knowing they did not know what loomed for him and them, saying, "You will drink the cup." Back in reality he informs them he doesn't decide who gets which seats in the kingdom banquets (10:39–40).

LIVING THE CROSS

As Jesus was angered with the disciples (10:14), so ten disciples become angry over the two brothers for their audacious quests for glory (10:41). What Jesus says next has been used aplenty in discussing *leader*ship but the passage is about *follower*ship or *disciple*ship. To make this about leaders, that is about who is at the top of the flow chart and who is in charge and who has authority, flies against the whole point: Jesus is teaching disciples, not about how to exercise their authority, power, or leadership, but what it means to follow the Jesus of the Cross. Having said that, *because* it is about *disciple*ship it pertains to *leader*ship. The best leaders are the best disciples of Jesus. Leadership begins (or dies) with followership.

To make the passage about leadership, then, is only a subtle form of being like James and John. Giving a quick glance to cities like Tiberias or Caesarea Maritima or Damascus or Rome, Jesus states that gentile rulers love to lord it over, that is, exercise power and authority over others. Their favorite term, used twice here, is "over" (10:42). But among Jesus' circle of followers, greatness is not measured by "over" but by "under," that is, by serving others (10:43–44). Jesus is the pure example. Though the "Son of Man," and one needs to think of Daniel 7, he did not come to be "over" others but to be "under" others by giving "his life as a ransom for many" (10:45).

Education for Jesus was about emulation and imitation of him. Who he was and is, what he did and does—those are what needs to be emulated by his followers. His mode of operation was not to be over people but to be under them in serving them. The Jesus of the Cross summons us to be disciples of the Cross.

QUESTIONS FOR REFLECTION AND APPLICATION

1. How is pursuing glory opposed to pursuing Jesus?

2. How does Jesus respond to the glory-seeking of James and John?

3. What is the difference between leadership and follower-ship? What characteristics are more important to Jesus?

4. Why do you think Jesus' followers were both astonished and afraid?

5. What have been some of your complex or contradictory emotions in your life of following Jesus?

JESUS OF THE CROSS: FOR OTHERS

Mark 10:46–52

⁴⁶ Then they came to Jericho. As Jesus and his disciples, together with a large crowd, were leaving the city, a blind man, Bartimaeus (which means "son of Timaeus"), was sitting by the roadside begging. ⁴⁷ When he heard that it was Jesus of Nazareth, he began to shout, "Jesus, Son of David, have mercy on me!"

⁴⁸ Many rebuked him and told him to be quiet, but he shouted all the more, "Son of David, have mercy on me!"

⁴⁹ Jesus stopped and said, "Call him."

So they called to the blind man, "Cheer up! On your feet! He's calling you."

⁵⁰ Throwing his cloak aside, he jumped to his feet and came to Jesus.

⁵¹ "What do you want me to do for you?" Jesus asked him.

The blind man said, "Rabbi, I want to see."

⁵² "Go," said Jesus, "your faith has healed you." Immediately he received his sight and followed Jesus along the road.

It's only one word in Greek, two words in English. Jesus asks the man, "What do you want me to do for you?" The English "for you" perfectly translates one simple Greek personal pronoun: *soi*. When I read this my eyes run up the page to the last words of our last passage: "for many." Jesus' life was a serving life for the benefit and redemption of others. He gave himself for others. His life was for others. The unleashing of kingdom redemption by Jesus, whether in Galilee or on the way up the path to Jerusalem, was for the benefit of others.

As Jesus and his disciples are leaving Jericho, they encounter a man "along the path" (cf. 4:4, 15) with a disability, that is, he had vision impairment (NIV: "blind"). This was not simply a physical disability but his social status and meaning in life were impacted by social perceptions. His name, Bartimaeus, means "son of honor," which is a socially challenging name for a disabled man. The man was noisy about his needs, and those who wanted respect for Jesus, like Peter in 8:32–33, urged him to be silent, which intensified his disability even more. Jesus counters the silencing and requests the man to come to him (10:50), at which time Jesus asks the "for you" question. The man's answer is as simple as it is socially significant: "Rabbi, I want to see" (10:51). Jesus heals the man, "he received his sight and followed," now with seeing eyes and a social status to match, "Jesus along the road" (10:52). How far he accompanied them is not clear, but the longer he stayed with Jesus the more of the Cross he would have seen.

Remember again our theme: the Jesus of the Cross calls people to a discipleship of the Cross. On the path to Jerusalem Jesus provides what could be called final teachings on discipleship. One of the most memorable was that Jesus, when assailed by the prospect of his impending, imminent brutal death at the hands of the socially sanctioned temple authorities and power-invested Roman leaders, pauses to heal a disabled man and sets him on the path of following him. Never too hurried to notice a person in need.

QUESTIONS FOR REFLECTION
AND APPLICATION

1. How did Jesus live out selfless service for others? (for you, *soi*)

2. In this study guide, McKnight often uses disability language. Had you thought before about the Gospels in terms of disability?

3. What is particularly significant about Jesus' pause to interact with Bartimaeus on the way to Jerusalem?

4. What might happen if you slowed your pace of life to make time for vulnerable people in need?

5. If Jesus asked you, "What do you want me to do for you?" what would you ask for?

JESUS OF THE CROSS: PROCLAMATION AND PRONOUNCEMENT

Mark 11:1–25

Proclamation

¹ As they approached Jerusalem and came to Bethphage and Bethany at the Mount of Olives, Jesus sent two of his disciples, ² saying to them, "Go to the village ahead of you, and just as you enter it, you will find a colt tied there, which no one has ever ridden. Untie it and bring it here. ³ If anyone asks you, 'Why are you doing this?' say, 'The Lord needs it and will send it back here shortly.' "

⁴ They went and found a colt outside in the street, tied at a doorway. As they untied it, ⁵ some people standing there asked, "What are you doing, untying that colt?" ⁶ They answered as Jesus had told them to, and the people let them go. ⁷ When they brought the colt to Jesus and threw their cloaks over it, he sat on it. ⁸ Many people spread their cloaks on the road, while others spread branches they had cut in the fields. ⁹ Those who went ahead and those who followed shouted,

> *"Hosanna!"*
> *"Blessed is he who comes in the name of the Lord!"*

*¹⁰ "Blessed is the coming kingdom of our father
     David!"*
"Hosanna in the highest heaven!"

*¹¹ Jesus entered Jerusalem and went into the temple courts. He
looked around at everything, but since it was already late, he went
out to Bethany with the Twelve.*

Pronouncement

*¹²The next day as they were leaving Bethany, Jesus was hun-
gry. ¹³ Seeing in the distance a fig tree in leaf, he went to find out if
it had any fruit. When he reached it, he found nothing but leaves,
because it was not the season for figs. ¹⁴ Then he said to the tree,
"May no one ever eat fruit from you again." And his disciples heard
him say it.*

*¹⁵ On reaching Jerusalem, Jesus entered the temple courts
and began driving out those who were buying and selling there.
He overturned the tables of the money changers and the benches
of those selling doves, ¹⁶ and would not allow anyone to carry
merchandise through the temple courts. ¹⁷ And as he taught
them, he said, "Is it not written: 'My house will be called a
house of prayer for all nations'? But you have made it 'a den
of robbers.'"*

*¹⁸ The chief priests and the teachers of the law heard this
and began looking for a way to kill him, for they feared him,
because the whole crowd was amazed at his teaching.*

*¹⁹ When evening came, Jesus and his disciples went out of
the city.*

*²⁰ In the morning, as they went along, they saw the fig tree withered
from the roots. ²¹ Peter remembered and said to Jesus, "Rabbi, look!
The fig tree you cursed has withered!"*

²² "Have faith in God," Jesus answered. ²³ "Truly I tell you, if anyone says to this mountain, 'Go, throw yourself into the sea,' and does not doubt in their heart but believes that what they say will happen, it will be done for them. ²⁴ Therefore I tell you, whatever you ask for in prayer, believe that you have received it, and it will be yours. ²⁵ And when you stand praying, if you hold anything against anyone, forgive them, so that your Father in heaven may forgive you your sins."*

Jesus taught about the kingdom and discipleship, both in synagogues and on the path, and he dispensed kingdom redemption from person to person. The crowds, both in Galilee and Judea, were attracted to him. The temple authorities in Jerusalem, under constant watch by the Roman authorities (Pilate, Tiberius through Sejanus), because they were hearing about Jesus from their agents (Pharisees, scribes), were wary of Jesus. *How* Jesus entered into the City in his last week and *what he did once there*, two events in today's passage, turned the tide of the temple authorities against Jesus. The entire week is a story of conflict, of the temple authorities searching how to apprehend him in private, and Jesus taking the public stage to take on his critics. The two actions of today's passage describe Jesus' deliberate provocations, one a prophetic act of *proclamation* and then the second a prophetic action of *pronouncement* of judgment. These two events usher us into the last week of Jesus (see sidebar on pp. 197–199).

PROCLAMATION

Jesus' act of riding, instead of walking, into Jerusalem is subversively designed to remind attentive observers, and the temple authorities were attentive, of Zechariah 9:9.

---

* The best ancient manuscripts do not contain Mark 11:26.

That Jesus does this to open up his Passover participation requires us to understand the event as an act of liberation by a liberating king. In that passage, Zechariah predicts judgment on surrounding nations and the entrance of a king into Jerusalem:

> 8 But I will encamp at my temple
>   to guard it against marauding forces.
> Never again will an oppressor overrun my people,
>   for now I am keeping watch.
> 9 Rejoice greatly, Daughter Zion!
>   Shout, Daughter Jerusalem!
> See, your king comes to you,
>   righteous and victorious,
> lowly and riding on a donkey,
>   on a colt, the foal of a donkey.
> 10 I will take away the chariots from Ephraim
>   and the warhorses from Jerusalem,
>   and the battle bow will be broken.
> He will proclaim peace to the nations.
>   His rule will extend from sea to sea
>   and from the River to the ends of the earth
>   (9:8–10).

This king will rule the world and, most noticeably, bring peace to the people of God. One cannot avoid attributing these words to the action of Jesus for one undeniable act: *he enters Jerusalem on a donkey*. The attentive see the donkey, they see crowds around him, and they see a claim to royalty, and then they connect that claim as public proclamation of Jesus as the king of Israel predicted by Zechariah. Ordinary, especially Roman, emperors enter cities they conquer with pomp that celebrates power. Jesus chooses not pomp and not power. He enters in humility when he mounts a donkey. He's anti-Rome. His kingdom is not a Roman kingdom. The donkey anticipates the Cross.

When the Maccabees regained control of Jerusalem, Simon Maccabee was a leading military commander who liberated villages in the land from the control of the Syrians (Seleucids). Simon himself entered Jerusalem in triumph, and here is a description of his entry:

> Those who were in the citadel at Jerusalem were prevented from going in and out to buy and sell in the country. So they were very hungry, and many of them perished from famine. Then they cried to Simon to make peace with them, and he did so. But he expelled them from there and cleansed the citadel from its pollutions. On the twenty-third day of the second month, in the one hundred seventy-first year, the Jews entered it with praise and palm branches, and with harps and cymbals and stringed instruments, and with hymns and songs, because a great enemy had been crushed and removed from Israel. Simon decreed that every year they should celebrate this day with rejoicing. He strengthened the fortifications of the temple hill alongside the citadel, and he and his men lived there (1 Maccabees 13:49–52).

One cannot imagine many in Jerusalem, especially at Passover, who do not know of Simon and his liberating victories and entry. The more they know about Simon the more they recognize Jesus' counter style: pomp vs. humility. Jesus subverts the way of power because he is Messiah of the Cross. Tim Gombis is right when he says Jesus' entry is an "anti-triumphal entry" (Gombis, *Mark*, 382).

The Last Week as Presented by the Gospels

(including Gospel of John only when it has a parallel to the Synoptics)

	Matthew	Mark	Luke	John
Arrival in Bethany				12:1
Entry in Jerusalem	21:1–11	11:1–10	19:29–44	12:12–19
Weeping			19:41	
Observes temple		11:11		
Returns to Bethany		11:11		
Curses fig tree	21:18–19	11:11–18		
Temple action	21:12–13	11:15–18	19:45–46 (47–48)	
Return to Bethany		11:19		
Fig tree	21:20–22	11:20–26		
Authority question	21:23–27	11:27–33	20:1–8	
Parable of two sons	21:28–32			
Parable of vineyard	21:33–46	12:1–12	20:9–19	
Parable of wedding	22:1–14			

(continued)

197

	Matthew	Mark	Luke	John
Taxes for Caesar	22:15–22	12:13–17	20:20–26	
Resurrection question	22:23–33	12:18–27	20:27–40	
Greatest command		12:28–34		
Whose son question	22:41–46	12:35–37	20:41–44	
Woes	23:1–39	12:38–40	20:45–47	
Widow's offering		12:41–44	21:1–4	
Prophesying on Olivet	24:1–36	13:1–32	21:5–36	
Days of Noah	24:37–41			
Ten Virgins	25:1–13			
Parable of bags of gold	25:14–30	13:33–37		
Parable of sheep & goats	25:31–46			
Summary			21:37–38	
Sanhedrin plot	26:1–5	14:1–2	22:1–2	
Mary anoints Jesus	26:6–13	14:3–9		12:2–8
Judas' plot	26:14–16	14:10–11	22:3–6	
Preparation	26:17–20	14:12–17	22:7–14	
Greatest question			22:24–30	

	Matthew	Mark	Luke	John
Judas identified	26:21–25	14:18–21	22:21–23	13:21–30
Last supper	26:26–29	14:22–25	22:15–20	
Singing	26:30	14:26		
Peter's denial predicted	26:31–35	14:27–31	22:31–38	13:36–38
Gethsemane prayer	26:36–46	14:32–42	22:39–46	
Arrest	26:47–56	14:43–52	22:47–53	18:2–12

John's Gospel has five chapters to conversation, instruction, and prayer (13–17).

Details of what will occur is foreknown by Jesus: from knowing the location of an unridden "colt" to knowing in advance its owner would surrender the colt to two of Jesus' closest followers. All of this, too, is staged by Jesus. Prophetic actions are planned before they are enacted. The perceptive "spread their cloaks on the road, while others spread branches they had cut in the fields" to welcome the entry of the king (11:4–8). Their words turn the event from something barely noticeable into something announced: "Hosanna" and "Blessed is he who comes" and "Blessed is the coming kingdom of our father David" proclaim to all that the man on the donkey is the future king of Israel. Jesus' action and their words spread quickly into the inner circles of the temple authorities.

Jesus attaches his provocative entry into Jerusalem to an evening stroll leading to a decision that what he planned next would need to wait for the next day. He leaves the City and walks to Bethany with the Twelve (11:11). His prophetic action has proclaimed who he is.

PRONOUNCEMENT

We get a mini-Markan sandwich at Mark 11:12–25. Mark surrounds Jesus' temple disturbance with the symbolic action of cursing a fig tree. They combine to form a graphic pronouncement of divine judgment on the temple establishment's corruptions. Jesus has now shifted his scene of operations from Galilee and the hills of Judea to the center of power. In doing this he stands up straight in front of the very ones most concerned about the Jesus movement.

The fig tree incident has two strikes against it. First, Jesus' hunger seems a weak reason for withering a fig tree. (This is not a tree hugger comment, though many have made such comments.) Second, it wasn't even the time for figs, so why would Jesus send dryness through a tree for what it couldn't produce until the fruit-bearing season arrived? Even though he was hungry, and even though it was not the season for figs, Jesus de-fruited the tree. The entire act, Jesus will explain the next day, was done as an acted oracle that pronounces judgment on the City, which will occur in 66–73 AD at the hands of the Romans. The fig tree is an image for Israel (Jeremiah 8:13), but perhaps even more an image of what will be a flourishing tree in the messianic era (Micah 4:4). On top of that, Jesus informed his disciples that their prayers for the impossible will be answered. In context, what the disciples would be praying for is the establishment of justice for what would be done by the end of the week. Theirs is to ask and to trust the good God and Father of Jesus. And, while they're praying, he adds that they are to forgive those who have something against them. I believe Jesus still has his imminent death at the hands of the powers in mind, and the disciples will be challenged to forgive the persecutors of Jesus and those who follow him.

Jesus' action in the temple, a fitting climax to Jesus'

routine tensions with the temple authorities, protests economic exploitation of the poor, and surely he knew this by experience in Galilee. Let me back up to explain a feature often neglected. The Pharisees, along with the teachers of the law (scribes) and at times Herodians, were sent to inspect Jesus. His popularity concerned them, but his charisma and powers made it difficult to oppose him. Those who sent the Pharisees were Jerusalem's temple authorities, and it is no small matter that at times what drove one of the concerns of the authorities was economic. Was Jesus stirring up an economic protest against heavy taxation? For the moment we need only to consider how important the poor were to Jesus. Zoom forward now to his noisy entrance and to his cursing of the fig tree. In the temple he cites two texts from two prophets who themselves had their own prophetic acts of resistance. Here Jesus reminds those watching his protest of exploiting the poor (see esp. Jeremiah 7:6, 9). One finds a similar protest of temple exploitation in the Dead Sea Scrolls. In these lines we hear a prediction of good priests to come when God redeems the true people of God, that is, we hear a prediction of the priests desired in the Qumran community:

> They must be careful to act according to the specifications of the Law for the era of wickedness, separating from corrupt people, avoiding filthy wicked lucre taken from what is vowed or consecrated to God or found in the Temple funds. They must not rob "the poor of God's people, making widows' wealth their booty and killing orphans" (Isaiah 10:2; from *Damascus Document* 6:14–17).

Tie this all into a tight knot now and here's what we get: as soon as Jesus gets into the temple courts, he defends the poor by protesting the exploitation of the poor by the temple authorities and at the same time pronounces divine judgment. They are not the last words of today's passage, but they are the words that turn the events into sinister activity: "The chief priests and the teachers of the law heard this and began looking for a way to kill him, for they feared him, because the whole crowd was amazed at his teaching" (Mark 11:18). From Mark 3:6 a plot has been underway in this Gospel to dispatch Jesus. Little did the Rome-appointed governor, Pilate, know his opponents would soon succeed, but that success would be turned into a massive mistake.

Two prophetic actions, each provoking attention and each shackling Jesus to charges of political chicanery, arrogance, and insurrection. In the first he acts out being a king, albeit a humble king, and the second embodies protest against the temple's exploitation of the poor, which protest becomes a pronouncement of judgment against the officials and the City. Jesus took one day to make his mark. He subverts the ways of Rome, the ways of the temple authorities, and in so subverting Jesus acts out what it means to be a Messiah of the Cross. Meanwhile, the disciples watch.

QUESTIONS FOR REFLECTION AND APPLICATION

1. The crowds were attracted to Jesus. If Jesus were incarnate amongst us today, do you think crowds would be as drawn to him?

2. How does Mark intensify the conflict in this passage?

3. How does Jesus draw on liberating and prophetic images as he moves toward the cross?

4. If Jesus came today, what are some actions that would represent prophetic, anti-imperial, liberating lordship in our culture in the same way he did upon entering Jerusalem?

5. What kind of actions could you take to protest the exploitation of the poor?

JESUS OF THE CROSS: RISKS WITH NO ADVANTAGES (1)

Mark 11:27–12:17

Authority

27 They arrived again in Jerusalem, and while Jesus was walking in the temple courts, the chief priests, the teachers of the law and the elders came to him. 28 "By what authority are you doing these things?" they asked. "And who gave you authority to do this?"

29 Jesus replied, "I will ask you one question. Answer me, and I will tell you by what authority I am doing these things. 30 John's baptism—was it from heaven, or of human origin? Tell me!"

31 They discussed it among themselves and said, "If we say, 'From heaven,' he will ask, 'Then why didn't you believe him?' 32 But if we say, 'Of human origin' . . ." (They feared the people, for everyone held that John really was a prophet.)

33 So they answered Jesus, "We don't know."

Jesus said, "Neither will I tell you by what authority I am doing these things."

History

12:1 Jesus then began to speak to them in parables: "A man planted a vineyard. He put a wall around it, dug a pit for the winepress and built a watchtower. Then he rented the vineyard to some farmers and moved to another place. 2 At harvest time he sent a servant to the tenants to collect from them some of the fruit of the vineyard. 3 But they seized him, beat him and sent him away empty-handed. 4 Then he sent another servant to them; they struck this man on the head and treated him shamefully. 5 He sent still another, and that one they killed. He sent many others; some of them they beat, others they killed.

6 "He had one left to send, a son, whom he loved. He sent him last of all, saying, 'They will respect my son.'

7 "But the tenants said to one another, 'This is the heir. Come, let's kill him, and the inheritance will be ours.' 8 So they took him and killed him, and threw him out of the vineyard.

9 "What then will the owner of the vineyard do? He will come and kill those tenants and give the vineyard to others. 10 Haven't you read this passage of Scripture:

> *" 'The stone the builders rejected*
> *   has become the cornerstone;*
> *11 the Lord has done this,*
> *   and it is marvelous in our eyes'?"*

12 Then the chief priests, the teachers of the law and the elders looked for a way to arrest him because they knew he had spoken the parable against them. But they were afraid of the crowd; so they left him and went away.

Complicity

13 Later they sent some of the Pharisees and Herodians to Jesus to catch him in his words. 14 They came to him and said, "Teacher, we know that you are a man of integrity. You aren't swayed by others, because you pay no attention to who they are; but you teach the way of God in accordance with the truth. Is it right to pay the imperial tax to Caesar or not? ¹⁵ *Should we pay or shouldn't we?"*

But Jesus knew their hypocrisy. "Why are you trying to trap me?" he asked. "Bring me a denarius and let me look at it."

¹⁶ *They brought the coin, and he asked them, "Whose image is this? And whose inscription?"*

"Caesar's," they replied.

¹⁷ *Then Jesus said to them, "Give back to Caesar what is Caesar's and to God what is God's." And they were amazed at him.*

Have you ever had to talk truth to power? Those who do weigh the risks against the advantages. The risks usually have to do with reputation, status, honor, pride, glory, income, family security, benefits, career, and future employment. The advantages, if one is realistic, are reducible to one: speaking truth, or even telling off the powers. Realism pushes the one talking truth to power to see that much is at stake and the chance of winning is very low, like picking the right numbers in a lottery. Try taking your concerns from your local community all the way up to your country's capitol. The risks get greater while the advantages grow slimmer.

Talk about speaking truth to power. In today's passage Jesus clashes with the following groups of leaders in Jerusalem: the chief priests, the teachers of the law, the elders, the Pharisees, and the Herodians (11:27; 12:12, 13). That is, with Rome-endorsed powers, the religious establishment, the expert law teachers, the inherited families, their popular agents known for their law observance, and those who represent Herod Antipas, who rules in Galilee. What Jesus risked was not employment or reputation; his life was on the line. Opposing the temple authorities, whoever represented them in these tussles with Jesus, could lead to charges before the Rome-endorsed governor, Pilate, who had the power of life and death.

Three themes rise to the level of risk in today's passage. Jesus is challenged about the source for his authority to be doing what he's doing; Jesus challenges right back by providing a parabolic retelling of Israel's history; and then Jesus is challenged about whether he is complicit with Caesar or with Caesar's opponents.

AUTHORITY

A triple layer of authority questions Jesus with a "By what authority?" and "Who gave you authority?" for what he was doing. What he was *doing* was entering the City to some fanfare and then protesting the temple authorities' exploitation of the poor. Good question, actually. Jesus decides to expand their question in order to get them to declare their beliefs about what he knows God is doing in Israel. So, he backs up to John the Baptist and asks them where his authority came from (11:27–30).

The triple layer of authority's deliberation leads them to conclude he's put them into a very clever either-or dilemma, and the authorities want no part of having to choose. This reminds of a few (pseudo) conversations many of us have observed. When some people are asked a very clear question, they choose not to answer it. Most observers think the choice not to answer the question is a way of not having to express what they don't want to get in trouble for. At times we may choose not to get in trouble, or we may choose that we won't participate in the gambit we are being pushed into by the question. But one suspects that many choose not to answer because their answer will not be acceptable. Will it be God or the people? The choice was theirs, and they passed the buck.

The triple authority answer is "We don't know" so Jesus

refuses to say "God" for the source for his authority. He chooses not to play their one-way conversation that they can take back to the temple inner rooms for a report. Instead of answering that question, he *actually does answer it* with a parable. In so doing, Jesus moves from a no-risk non-answer to a risky answer with deadly possibilities.

History

The short stories of Jesus, or parables or analogies, press listeners into an imaginative world where life turns out differently. An entrepreneur plants grape vines, constructs a watchtower, and builds a winepress to produce wine from his vineyard. (A vineyard was a common trope for Israel. See Isaiah 5.) Instead of farming it himself, he farms it out and moves away and plans on collecting his dough at harvest season (12:1). He first sends a slave (NIV plays it nice with "servant") but the tenants beat the slave; then he sent another slave whom they treated "shamefully"; then another whom they killed. Amazingly, he next sends his "son, whom he loved" (sounds like the Father's words at the baptism and transfiguration; 1:11; 9:7), but they murdered him too (12:2–8). Morna Hooker's observation pierces the inner fabric of Jesus' parable: "The behaviour of the tenants seems absurdly foolish, but that, of course, is the point of the story!" (Hooker, *Mark*, 274).

The parable tells a history of how the people of God have responded to the prophets sent from God. This telling of history, however, ends with the special son being murdered. So, Jesus asks the triple authorities what the entrepreneur should do. But before they answer, Jesus answers his own question by appealing to Psalm 118:22–23. Instead of a son, there is a "stone" that is rejected by builders that becomes the "cornerstone," and the impact of that act was amazing (Mark

12:9–11). The end of the tenants, death, corresponds to the cursing of the fig tree. Divine judgment looms.

Jesus' silence in the previous passage now gets matched by the silence of the triple authorities (12:12). They knew his story about history was a story about their participation in opposition to the prophets of God, with their rejection of Jesus corresponding to rejecting God's Son. Instead of surrendering to the work of God in John and in Jesus, they "looked for a way to arrest him." They fear the crowds, who have been the problem from the beginning because they see what Jesus does and they hear his sayings and conclude Jesus has been sent from God. So, in silence they go absent from the presence of Jesus. They would not risk their answer because there were for them no advantages.

COMPLICITY

Their fear of the crowds, they surmise, can be taken care of by the Pharisees, whom the crowds also love. So they send the Pharisees, along with Rome's representatives, the Herodians, and this intensifies the risk for Jesus.* Their job was to ask a riddling question with significant risk in order to trap Jesus. Using the skill of buttering-up, they affirm Jesus as a "man of integrity," or a true man who unbiasedly teaches the truth (12:14). Now the buttering-up turns into the trap: Is it observant to "pay the imperial tax to Caesar or not? Should we pay or shouldn't we?" (12:14). When it comes to authority, who has more than Caesar?

Jesus had forced the powers to decide on John's authority, so they now force Jesus to declare if he is pro- or anti-Rome, if he's pro-subversives or pro-power. We must assume the

---

* There is so much alike in this passage to the passage in Luke I have edited what I wrote there.

Herodians were all-in for taxes to Caesar. As agents of the temple authorities, the Pharisees, too, were pro-poll taxes to Caesar. Jesus discerns what the NIV calls their "hypocrisy" (12:15). That is, he knew their question was pretentious. He asks for a coin, obtains one, flips it in his fingers and plays a first century heads-or-tails game with "Whose image is this? And whose inscription?" Their answer for the coin showing up heads is the right one, "Caesar's" (12:16).

His answer unravels their riddle, one that poses the law of taxation against the law of God. So he says, "Give back to Caesar what is Caesar's, and to God what is God's" (12:17). Do they comprehend his riddle? If he had said pay taxes, the ordinary people who love Jesus would have wondered about the politics of Jesus and John; if he had said not to pay taxes, they were with him but big trouble would follow. To pay taxes declares allegiance to Caesar. Use of the coin, too, exhibits a violation of the commandment about making images (Exodus 20:4), and if it is the coin most think, it inscribed Caesar as "divine augustus." Is giving the coin back a summons to avoid the idolatry? Jesus, you observe, does not have a coin himself. Is he saying give the filthy stuff back to Rome and learn to serve God apart from images? If so, the riddle poses a choice: Either God or Caesar. Complicity either way.

Jesus' words are not about separation of church and state—give God's money to God and Caesar's money to Caesar. It is a riddle that rhetorically reaches into their hearts for a decision. His answer subverts their question and challenges their allegiance to Caesar. Jesus and John or Rome? In Luke's Gospel, we read that some who heard Jesus would soon put forward allegations against Jesus because he "opposes payment of taxes to Caesar" (Luke 23:2). That statement deserves to be part of how we understand the riddle of Jesus, and I believe it shows that Jesus subverts taxes that exploit the poor. Once again, Jesus presses against the temple authorities for their economic injustices. His riddling answer "amazed" them (12:17).

Jesus is not complicit with Rome. He's complicit with what God is doing from John the Baptist on, with the way of the Cross, and with the way of justice for the poor. His answer risked his life. The disciples are watching. We hear not a peep from them, but taking it in, they realize the way of the Cross comes with great risks.

Questions for Reflection and Application

1. Which authorities does Jesus challenge?

2. How does Jesus employ parables in his challenge to powerbrokers?

3. Why do you think the Pharisees were popular with the people?

4. Have you ever had to talk truth to power? Were there any advantages or just risks?

5. How might you live out an anti-power stance in your world?

JESUS OF THE CROSS: RISKS WITH NO ADVANTAGES (2)

Mark 12:18–44

Eternity

[18] Then the Sadducees, who say there is no resurrection, came to him with a question. [19] "Teacher," they said, "Moses wrote for us that if a man's brother dies and leaves a wife but no children, the man must marry the widow and raise up offspring for his brother. [20] Now there were seven brothers. The first one married and died without leaving any children. [21] The second one married the widow, but he also died, leaving no child. It was the same with the third. [22] In fact, none of the seven left any children. Last of all, the woman died too. [23] At the resurrection whose wife will she be, since the seven were married to her?"

[24] Jesus replied, "Are you not in error because you do not know the Scriptures or the power of God? [25] When the dead rise, they will neither marry nor be given in marriage; they will be like the angels in heaven. [26] Now about the dead rising—have you not read in the Book of Moses, in the account of the burning bush, how God said to him, 'I am the God of Abraham, the God of Isaac, and the God of

Jacob'? [27] *He is not the God of the dead, but of the living. You are badly mistaken!"*

Morality

[28] *One of the teachers of the law came and heard them debating. Noticing that Jesus had given them a good answer, he asked him, "Of all the commandments, which is the most important?"*

[29] *"The most important one," answered Jesus, "is this: 'Hear, O Israel: The Lord our God, the Lord is one.* [30] *Love the Lord your God with all your heart and with all your soul and with all your mind and with all your strength.'* [31] *The second is this: 'Love your neighbor as yourself.' There is no commandment greater than these."*

[32] *"Well said, teacher," the man replied. "You are right in saying that God is one and there is no other but him.* [33] *To love him with all your heart, with all your understanding and with all your strength, and to love your neighbor as yourself is more important than all burnt offerings and sacrifices."*

[34] *When Jesus saw that he had answered wisely, he said to him, "You are not far from the kingdom of God." And from then on no one dared ask him any more questions.*

Identity

[35] *While Jesus was teaching in the temple courts, he asked, "Why do the teachers of the law say that the Messiah is the son of David?* [36] *David himself, speaking by the Holy Spirit, declared:*

> " 'The Lord said to my Lord:
>   "Sit at my right hand
> until I put your enemies
>   under your feet." '

[37] *David himself calls him 'Lord.' How then can he be his son?"*
The large crowd listened to him with delight.

Celebrity

38 As he taught, Jesus said, "Watch out for the teachers of the law. They like to walk around in flowing robes and be greeted with respect in the marketplaces, 39 and have the most important seats in the synagogues and the places of honor at banquets. 40 They devour widows' houses and for a show make lengthy prayers. These men will be punished most severely."

Poverty

41 Jesus sat down opposite the place where the offerings were put and watched the crowd putting their money into the temple treasury. Many rich people threw in large amounts. 42 But a poor widow came and put in two very small copper coins, worth only a few cents.

43 Calling his disciples to him, Jesus said, "Truly I tell you, this poor widow has put more into the treasury than all the others. 44 They all gave out of their wealth; but she, out of her poverty, put in everything—all she had to live on."

Some people rise to the occasion of a controversy. They like the antagonisms. In fact, some look forward to the tension and approach it as an opportunity to win. Others are conflict-avoidant and non-confrontational. Both can grow from conflicts, and both can be deformed by it. Some go into full-fight mode while others grow passive and miss the opportunity to exercise their own agency. A full reading of the Gospels reveals Jesus as balanced between withdrawal from the tension and at other times taking a stand in the face of opponents. In the last week Jesus took issue with one group of Jerusalem's leaders after another.

In today's passage Jesus clashes with the following groups of leaders in Jerusalem: the elite family network of priests in Jerusalem, that is, the Sadducees, and then a teacher of the law (12:18, 28). But then Jesus delights the crowds when he proposes a riddle about David's and his own identity, which is followed by a warning about the ambition for celebrity status, all of which is wrapped up with the amazing sketch of the widow's offering.

ETERNITY

A contemporary historian, Josephus, observes the same, saying of the Sadducees that they believe "the soul perishes with the body" and that they like to argue about theology (*Antiquities* 18.16). That they denied the resurrection is both commonplace for historians and explicitly stated in today's passage when Mark writes "who say there is no resurrection" (Mark 12:18). Jesus did, and in believing in the resurrection he sided with the Pharisees against the Sadducees. Paul created a tumult over the differences between Pharisees and Sadducees some years later (Acts 23:6–8).

The Sadducees spin a contradiction for those who believe in a resurrection. A woman had married, in complete observance of the law of what is called "levirate marriage" (Deuteronomy 25:5–6), seven brothers who died in succession. In the Age to Come ("At the resurrection" in 12:23), they ask him, "Whose wife will she be?" Many Jews imagined the Age to Come in physical, familial, and social terms. The implication is that belief in a resurrection would make God's laws nonsensical.

Jesus responds by affirming Scripture and the "power of God" (12:24). Then Jesus says something that draws differing interpretations. He says, "When the dead rise, they will neither marry nor be given in marriage; they will be like the angels in heaven" (12:25). Jesus may be saying in the kingdom of God no one will be married because they, being like angels (which the Sadducees don't believe in either), will be immortal. Or, he may be more precisely saying there will be *no new marriages* in heaven but present-day families will remain intact. Mark reads "neither marry nor be given in marriage" (12:25). Read carefully it can be seen for what it says: it only claims there will be no *new* marriages. The second option is more likely than the first because not only are families intact but angels are not uniformly sexless in Judaism (notice Genesis 6:4). (I discuss this in my book *The Heaven Promise*, 162–170.) You may indeed wonder if the second option answers the Sadducees' question. Their question is answered when Jesus mentions God's saying he was the God of Abraham, Isaac, and Jacob. If God is still their God, then they are alive, and if they are alive, there's an anticipation of resurrection already in Exodus—or at least life after death (Exodus 3:6; Mark 12:26–27).

It's probably a little cheeky for us to say now "Next!" But how the text presents the events one after another.

MORALITY

At the time of Jesus the "teachers of the law" knew there were 613 commandments (commands, prohibitions) in the Law of Moses, and there was a discussion about morality that went a bit like this: *If we reduce the laws to the single most important, which would it be?* Or, *which of the commands explains all the others?* We read in a much later source, the *Babylonian Talmud* (Shabbat 31a), the following account where a debate like this occurs between the most important two rabbis at the time of Jesus:

> There was **another incident involving one gentile who came before Shammai** and said to Shammai: **Convert me on condition that you teach me the entire Torah while I am standing on one foot.** Shammai **pushed him** away **with the builder's cubit in his hand.** This was a common

measuring stick and Shammai was a builder by trade. The same gentile **came before Hillel. He converted him and said to him: That which is hateful to you do not do to another; that is the entire Torah, and the rest is its interpretation. Go study** (see For Further Reading for link).

If this represents anything like the time of Jesus, Hillel and Jesus were very close to one another. Jesus was for reducing the law to its basics, and he turns to the positive form and makes it two commands. Essentially, love God and love others, and he combines Deuteronomy 6:4–5 with Leviticus 19:18 (Mark 12:29–31). I call this the "Jesus Creed" because it is a creed-like statement of Jesus' teachings about morality. I repeat these three verses in Mark often (see my book *The Jesus Creed*).

The Jesus Creed in the New Testament

For the entire law is fulfilled in keeping this one command: "Love your neighbor as yourself" (Galatians 5:14).

[9] The commandments, "You shall not commit adultery," "You shall not murder," "You shall not steal," "You shall not covet," and whatever other command there may be, are summed up in this one command: "Love your neighbor as yourself." [10] Love does no harm to a neighbor. Therefore love is the fulfillment of the law (Romans 13:9–10).

If you really keep the royal law found in Scripture, "Love your neighbor as yourself," you are doing right (James 2:8).

Noticeably, for the first time in these conflict situations, one of the leaders in Jerusalem agrees with Jesus. The scribe's "Well said" affirms Jesus and the scribe echoes the prophets when he says his teaching those two commands are "more important than all burnt offerings and sacrifices" (12:33). Jesus affirms him right back with "You are not far from the kingdom of God" (12:34), but that ends their challenging of Jesus.

Back to the crowds.

IDENTITY

The next section opens by telling us Jesus had a question, but it does not tell us to whom he asked the question until verse thirty-seven, where we read about a "large crowd" who "listened to him with delight." Jesus' question riddles again, asking "Why do the teachers of the law," that is, those who had just challenged Jesus about the greatest commandment, "say the Messiah is the son of David?" (12:35). The title "*son* of David" refers to the Messiah but get a good grip on the term "son." Jesus turns back to David's own words in Psalm 110:1, adding "The Lord said to *my Lord*." David's own view of the Messiah is that the Messiah is his Lord. In that psalm David refers to God as Lord and then calls the Messiah his "Lord." Which leads to the riddling question: How can the Messiah be both David's Lord and his son (apart from preexistence)? Or, perhaps, how can the Lord be David's Lord and David's son?

The crowds love it because they perceive Jesus has out-riddled the riddling Sadducees and out-challenged the challenging teachers of the law.

CELEBRITY

Apparently Jesus, still teaching the crowds—Mark didn't have paragraph or header divisions—warns them about the "teachers of the law" (12:38). That group of scholars goes lush with the trappings of celebrity, things like "flowing robes" and being recognized as a somebody in public places, and "the most important seats in the synagogues" and having "places of honor at banquets" (12:38–39). Plus, they parade their piety when praying (12:40).

Jesus exaggerates a common reality for a reason: he wants the crowds to dissociate themselves from the scribes because Jesus knows they are far from the ways of God. He wants the crowds to be drawn in his kingdom mission, so he discredits the teachers of the law as fame-seekers instead of the true people of God.

POVERTY

Jesus positioned himself so he could spot those donating alms and offerings to the temple (12:41). True to his concern with the poor and with the economic exploitation of the temple authorities, Jesus spots the glaring gulf between the rich people donating many coins (NIV has "large amounts") into the "temple treasury" at the same time a "poor widow" dropped in "two small copper coins" (12:41–42). Jesus' word for his disciples, now distinguished from the crowds of 12:37, is that the poor widow—notice his language of quantity—donated "more than all the others" (12:43). She donated out of her "poverty" and they must have been giving some excess of their abundance. To be pointed, he says she gave "all she had to live on" (12:44). Ever attentive to the piety of the poor, Jesus instructs his disciples that her giving was generously disproportionate to her poverty while the rich fellas' donations were disproportionate to their wealth. One can ask if this text is about generosity. I don't think so. More than anything else, this text reveals status-mongering by the wealthy, whom the poor widow shows up in her simple faithfulness to worship.

QUESTIONS FOR REFLECTION AND APPLICATION

1. How do both Paul and Jesus play off of the differences between the Pharisees and the Saducees?

2. Do you think there will be new marriages in heaven? Will existing marriages still mean something?

3. How does Jesus boil down the most important commandments compared to other religious leaders of his time?

4. What do the crowds think of Jesus' rhetorical skills?

5. Where and how do you perceive status-mongering among the wealthy in your community?

FOR FURTHER READING

Josephus, *Antiquities of the Jews,* Loeb Classical Library (trans. L.H. Feldman; Cambridge, Mass.: Harvard University Press, 1981), citing from volume 9, p. 13.

Scot McKnight, *The Jesus Creed: Loving God, Loving Others* (Brewster, MA: Paraclete, 2014).

On Shabbat 31a, see https://www.sefaria.org/Shabbat .31a.6?lang=bi&with=all&lang2=en

Scot McKnight, *The Heaven Promise,* (Colorado Springs, CO: Waterbrook, 2016).

JESUS OF THE CROSS: AN APOCALYPSE OF DIVINE JUDGMENT

Mark 13:1–37

Context

¹ As Jesus was leaving the temple, one of his disciples said to him, "Look, Teacher! What massive stones! What magnificent buildings!"

² "Do you see all these great buildings?" replied Jesus. "Not one stone here will be left on another; every one will be thrown down."

*³ As Jesus was sitting on the Mount of Olives opposite the temple, Peter, James, John and Andrew asked him privately, ⁴ "Tell us, **when** will these things happen? And what will be **the sign** that they are all about to be fulfilled?"*

When

⁵ Jesus said to them: "Watch out that no one deceives you. ⁶ Many will come in my name, claiming, 'I am he,' and will deceive many. ⁷ When you hear of wars and rumors of wars, do not be alarmed. Such things must happen, but the end is still to come. ⁸ Nation will rise against nation, and kingdom against kingdom. There will be earthquakes in various places, and famines. These are the beginning of birth pains.

⁹ "You must be on your guard. You will be handed over to the local councils and flogged in the synagogues. On account of me you will stand before governors and kings as witnesses to them. ¹⁰ And the gospel must first be preached to all nations. ¹¹ Whenever you are arrested and brought to trial, do not worry beforehand about what to say. Just say whatever is given you at the time, for it is not you speaking, but the Holy Spirit.

¹² "Brother will betray brother to death, and a father his child. Children will rebel against their parents and have them put to death. ¹³ Everyone will hate you because of me, but the one who stands firm to the end will be saved.

¹⁴ "When you see 'the abomination that causes desolation' standing where it does not belong—let the reader understand—then let those who are in Judea flee to the mountains. ¹⁵ Let no one on the housetop go down or enter the house to take anything out. ¹⁶ Let no one in the field go back to get their cloak. ¹⁷ How dreadful it will be in those days for pregnant women and nursing mothers! ¹⁸ Pray that this will not take place in winter, ¹⁹ because those will be days of distress unequaled from the beginning, when God created the world, until now—and never to be equaled again.

²⁰ "If the Lord had not cut short those days, no one would survive. But for the sake of the elect, whom he has chosen, he has shortened them. ²¹ At that time if anyone says to you, 'Look, here is the Messiah!' or, 'Look, there he is!' do not believe it. ²² For false messiahs and false prophets will appear and perform signs and wonders to deceive, if possible, even the elect. ²³ So be on your guard; I have told you everything ahead of time.

Sign

²⁴ "But in those days, following that distress,

> " 'the sun will be darkened,
>   and the moon will not give its light;

^{25} *the stars will fall from the sky,*
   and the heavenly bodies will be shaken.'

^{26} *"At that time people will see the Son of Man coming in clouds with great power and glory. ^{27} And he will send his angels and gather his elect from the four winds, from the ends of the earth to the ends of the heavens.*

When

^{28} *"Now learn this lesson from the fig tree: As soon as its twigs get tender and its leaves come out, you know that summer is near. ^{29} Even so, when you see these things happening, you know that it is near, right at the door. ^{30} Truly I tell you, this generation will certainly not pass away until all these things have happened. ^{31} Heaven and earth will pass away, but my words will never pass away.*

^{32} *"But about that day or hour no one knows, not even the angels in heaven, nor the Son, but only the Father. ^{33} Be on guard! Be alert! You do not know when that time will come. ^{34} It's like a man going away: He leaves his house and puts his servants in charge, each with their assigned task, and tells the one at the door to keep watch.*

^{35} *"Therefore keep watch because you do not know when the owner of the house will come back—whether in the evening, or at midnight, or when the rooster crows, or at dawn. ^{36} If he comes suddenly, do not let him find you sleeping. ^{37} What I say to you, I say to everyone: 'Watch!'"*

There is a conventional reading of this passage, and the whole needs to be read together, that understands it as a *future* description of the rebuilding of the temple in Jerusalem as well as the rapture of the saints. In the history of the church most have read this passage as Jesus predicting the destruction of the temple in the battle with Rome between

66–73 AD. I agree with the common view in the history of church, but that does not mean the passage is without value for discipleship today.

EXPLAINING THE PREDICTIONS

A specific context prompts the entire chapter. A disciple, as many who visited Jerusalem observed, remarks about the "massive stones" and "magnificent buildings" (13:1). I have walked along a massive stone underneath the current temple complex just north of the so-called Wailing Wall. The size of that one stone beggars description and forces one to wonder how such a colossal piece could have been moved from a stone quarry north of the City. Josephus, on the basis of personal observations, writes about the magnificence of the temple:

> Now the outward face of the temple in its front wanted nothing that was likely to surprise either men's minds or their eyes, for it was covered all over the plates of gold of great weight, and, at the first rising of the sun, reflected back a very fiery splendor, and made those who forced themselves to look upon it to turn their eyes away, just as they would have done at the sun's own rays. 223 (5.5.6) But this temple appeared to strangers, when they were at a distance, like a mountain covered with snow; for, as to those parts of it that were not gilt, they were exceeding white (*War* 5.222–223).

The disciple's observation to Jesus about the temple leads Jesus to answer him with a set-up question ("Do you see all these great buildings?") followed by a stunning prediction: "Not one stone here will be left on another; every one will be thrown down" (13:2). The "not one" expresses hyperbolically a toppling of the stones and edifices atop the massive stone complex on which the temple was built. The massive stones under it all were not moved.

His prediction of the destruction of the temple prompts four disciples to ask him privately two questions. The question of When and the question about the Sign. I have designated those sections in the translation above and want to explain each now.

WHEN

The word "when" appears in the NIV at 13:4, 7, 14, 29, 33, and 35. Add in other time indicators, like "will be" or "that time" or "those days" or "until" and you have lots of language that answered the very question the disciples asked. Jesus overtly states he *does not know the precise "day or hour"* (13:32) *but he does know some indicators* so I sketch each.

First, some will claim to be Messiah ("I am he" in 13:6) in a way that leads to deception. Second, "wars and rumors of war" occur and natural disasters, which Jesus calls the "beginnings of birth pains" (13:7–8). Third, the followers of Jesus will experience various forms of persecution as the gospel spreads throughout the Roman empire (13:9–13). Fourth, a particular moment occurs when the "abomination of desolation," predicted back in Daniel 9:27; 11:31; and 12:11; appears in the temple (13:14). Josephus describes an event that fits the bill of Daniel of an idolatrous act in the temple:

> And now the Romans, upon the flight of the seditious into the city, and upon the burning of the holy house itself, and of all the buildings round about it, brought their ensigns to the temple, and set them over against its eastern gate; and there did they offer sacrifices to them, and there did they make Titus imperator, with the greatest acclamations of joy (*War* 6.316).

Some claiming to be Messiah is repeated (Mark 13:20–23). Fifth, the signs (see below) will occur within a generation, that is, by about 70 AD (13:30). Jesus' predictions are not unlike what Josephus describes in his famous book on the *The Jewish War* with the Romans. Here are but two examples, the first from temple massacres and the second of those throughout the whole city:

> . . . for those darts that were thrown by the engines came with that force, that they went all over the buildings, and reached as far as the altar, and the temple itself, and fell upon the priests, and those that were about the sacred offices; insomuch that in any persons who came thither with great zeal from the ends of the earth, to offer sacrifices at this celebrated place, which was esteemed holy by all mankind, fell down before their own sacrifices themselves, and sprinkled that altar which was venerable among all men, both Greeks and Barbarians, with their own blood; till the dead bodies of strangers were mingled together with those of their own country, and those of profane persons with those of the priests, and the blood of all sorts of dead carcasses stood in lakes in the holy courts themselves (*War* 5.16–18).

> Nor was there any place in the city that had no dead bodies in it, but what was entirely covered with those that were killed either by the famine or the rebellion; and all was full of the dead bodies of such as had perished, either by that sedition or by that famine (*War* 6.369).

There is very little that reaches the depths of Josephus' descriptions of massacres and tragedies and violence and bloodshed.

The fifth point mentioned above absolutely means what Jesus predicts here is not something that *will* happen but that *has already happened*. Josephus' descriptions confirm it. Jesus revealed that what he was predicting about the toppling of the temple was to occur within the span of a generation. Unless one is prepared to argue Jesus just got it wrong, this utterly clear statement by Jesus needs to have a strong influence for how we read the sign, to which we now turn.

SIGN

Following the "distress" (13:24; KJV had "tribulation") of those four indicators of the time when the temple would be set ablaze, Jesus predicts the sign, or at least the preliminaries to the sign, but he does so by quoting from Isaiah 13:10 and 34:4 with at least an echo of Joel 2:10. Those verses refer to cosmic disturbances, and such images can be picked up by other Jewish writers to describe God's judgment. So, *1 Enoch*, a famous apocalyptic text in the Jewish world, says "All the luminaries shall faint with great fear; the whole earth shall faint and tremble and panic" (102:2; Charlesworth).

The sign is nothing less than the "Son of Man coming in clouds with great power and glory." (Matthew 24:30 explicitly identifies the Son of Man coming as the sign.) Attending the Son of Man will be the commissioning of angels to "gather his elect" from the whole world (Mark 13:26–27). The gathering here most likely refers to the gospel mission work throughout the whole world (as in 13:10). With the "Son of Man coming" Jesus refers back to Daniel 7:13–14. Pause now for a major shift in reading this passage. Something very important happens and I cannot emphasize this enough because of the conventional reading of Mark 13. The "coming" of Daniel 7 *is not a descent but an ascent from earth to the presence of the Ancient of Days.* Ascents describe triumph, divine reception and welcome, following a victory over sin and evil. Here are Daniel's words, and I have italicized the important words picked up by Jesus in Mark 13, and underlined words indicating an ascent:

> In my vision at night I looked, and there before me was one like a son of man, coming with the clouds of heaven. <u>He approached the Ancient of Days and was led into his presence</u>. He was given authority, glory and sovereign power; all nations and peoples of every language worshiped him. His dominion is an everlasting dominion that will not pass away, and his kingdom is one that will never be destroyed (Daniel 7:13–14).

In Daniel the son of man rises to rule over the world. Jesus' words about the asked-about sign point them to the day when Jesus rises to the Throne Room, not to a Second Coming to earth, and not to a rapture of the saints into the skies.

You would not surprise me if you are mutteringly wondering what event this "coming" refers to. It could, as some have suggested, refer to his resurrection and ascension, but since the rest of this chapter is all about the destruction of Jerusalem in 66–73 AD, it is more likely Jesus chooses Daniel 7's triumphal ascent to the day when God judges Jerusalem's temple authorities for their corruption. The Bible and Jewish literature encourage us to think of Rome's destruction of Jerusalem as a judgment against injustices and corruptions.

LIVING THE INSTRUCTIONS

The disciples asked When and about a Sign, but Jesus weaves into his answers to both instructions for how to live through the turbulent times of the destruction of Jerusalem. The front-page news is disciples will suffer (13:9–13). What Jesus said to them then has life for us today. As they had to face opposition to the gospel, so we may too. Several discipleship words raise their hands to grab our attention. I have narrowed them to *observation with discernment* (13:5, 7, 9, 33, 35), *resilient allegiance to Jesus* (13:13, with 13:21), and having enough common sense to *flee* (13:14).

A word about each. In the midst of opposition to the gospel, to Jesus, and to his kingdom vision, disciples will have seen how Jesus discerned the realities of this world. But Jesus warns against using events to predict the future. Instead of observing Putin crank up his tyranny, the believer can perceive the evil one destroying human lives and flourishing societies the way the Wild Things of Babylon do in Revelation. All day long we can observe the world around us and ask God for the kind of discernment that perceives the inner workings of God, and we can see natural disasters as warnings of final judgment. God is for truth, for justice, for peace, for love, for holiness, for following in the way of Jesus, for sacrificial service for others, and on and on. Where the world pushes back or turns such virtues aside, we discern, not the reluctant, providential hand of God but the ways of opposition to God.

Furthermore, we are called to resilient allegiance in the midst of suffering and opposition. The NIV has "stands firm," while other translations, like the ESV and NRSVue have "endures." The Greek word is *hypomenō*, and this term often refers to forming a resilient, steady, and faithful allegiance to Jesus and the way of the Cross. The word sometimes means to stay somewhere, as Jesus did in the temple at twelve (Luke 2:43). Paul uses the term just as Jesus does in Mark 13 when he says, "patient in affliction" (Romans 12:12), and he says love "perseveres" (1 Corinthians 13:7). He will later say to Timothy that "if we endure, we will also reign with him" (2 Timothy 2:12). The idea of resilient allegiance formed into an early Christian virtue as communities of faith learned to handle opposition (James 1:12; 1 Peter 2:20). Jesus was no idealist. When the war in Jerusalem ramps up, he tells his disciples to flee the city and go into hiding—just as Jesus has himself withdrawn as part of his strategy for the kingdom mission.

What Jesus does not exhort his disciples to do is start speculating about the future. Which is how many Christians treat Mark 13. Instead of asking questions about when it will happen or who will do what that is found in this chapter, Jesus predicts the future for the disciples so they comprehend the reality of future judgment and live in light of that future in the now. If he doesn't know the precise when, neither do his disciples. Theirs is not an escapist mentality, but a discipleship opportunity to live faithfully. If we give numbers some weight, the emphasis of Jesus is observation with discernment. He wants his followers to see what is happening, to remember what he has said and to discern the times. And in discerning they will know how to be resilient in their discipleship.

QUESTIONS FOR REFLECTION AND APPLICATION

1. Given the massive size and splendor of the Temple, how do you think the disciples processed Jesus' words about its destruction?

2. How does the shift from descent to ascent impact your understanding of the Daniel passage?

3. What does it mean to stay allegiant to Jesus in the face of suffering?

4. How might you grow in your resilient allegiance?

5. How can you discern signs that might help your resilience grow?

FOR FURTHER READING

Josephus, *War of the Jews*, cited from the software program of Accordance, Oak Tree Software, an edited version of William Whiston's translation.
Old Testament Pseudepigrapha, ed. J.H.Charlesworth, 2 volumes (New Haven: Yale University Press, 1983). The text of 1 Enoch is in volume 1.

JESUS OF THE CROSS: ANTICIPATION OF THE CROSS

Mark 14:1–31

1

¹ Now the Passover and the Festival of Unleavened Bread were only two days away, and the chief priests and the teachers of the law were scheming to arrest Jesus secretly and kill him. ² "But not during the festival," they said, "or the people may riot."

³ While he was in Bethany, reclining at the table in the home of Simon the Leper, a woman came with an alabaster jar of very expensive perfume, made of pure nard. She broke the jar and poured the perfume on his head.

⁴ Some of those present were saying indignantly to one another, "Why this waste of perfume? ⁵ It could have been sold for more than a year's wages and the money given to the poor." And they rebuked her harshly.

⁶ "Leave her alone," said Jesus. "Why are you bothering her? She has done a beautiful thing to me ⁷ The poor you will always have with you, and you can help them any time you want. But you will not always have me. ⁸ She did what she could. She poured perfume on my body beforehand to prepare for my burial. ⁹ Truly I tell you, wherever the gospel is preached throughout the world, what she has done will also be told, in memory of her."

¹⁰ Then Judas Iscariot, one of the Twelve, went to the chief priests to betray Jesus to them. ¹¹ They were delighted to hear this and promised to give him money. So he watched for an opportunity to hand him over.

2

¹² On the first day of the Festival of Unleavened Bread, when it was customary to sacrifice the Passover lamb, Jesus' disciples asked him, "Where do you want us to go and make preparations for you to eat the Passover?"

¹³ So he sent two of his disciples, telling them, "Go into the city, and a man carrying a jar of water will meet you. Follow him. ¹⁴ Say to the owner of the house he enters, 'The Teacher asks: Where is my guest room, where I may eat the Passover with my disciples?' ¹⁵ He will show you a large room upstairs, furnished and ready. Make preparations for us there."

¹⁶ The disciples left, went into the city and found things just as Jesus had told them. So they prepared the Passover.

¹⁷ When evening came, Jesus arrived with the Twelve. ¹⁸ While they were reclining at the table eating, he said, "Truly I tell you, one of you will betray me—one who is eating with me."

¹⁹ They were saddened, and one by one they said to him, "Surely you don't mean me?"

²⁰ "It is one of the Twelve," he replied, "one who dips bread into the bowl with me. ²¹ The Son of Man will go just as it is written about him. But woe to that man who betrays the Son of Man! It would be better for him if he had not been born."

²² While they were eating, Jesus took bread, and when he had given thanks, he broke it and gave it to his disciples, saying, "Take it; this is my body."

²³ Then he took a cup, and when he had given thanks, he gave it to them, and they all drank from it.

²⁴ "This is my blood of the covenant, which is poured out for many," he said to them. ²⁵ "Truly I tell you, I will not drink again from the fruit of the vine until that day when I drink it new in the kingdom of God."

3

²⁶ When they had sung a hymn, they went out to the Mount of Olives.

²⁷ "You will all fall away," Jesus told them, "for it is written:

" 'I will strike the shepherd,
        and the sheep will be scattered.'

²⁸ But after I have risen, I will go ahead of you into Galilee."

²⁹ Peter declared, "Even if all fall away, I will not."

³⁰ "Truly I tell you," Jesus answered, "today—yes, tonight—before the rooster crows twice you yourself will disown me three times."

³¹ But Peter insisted emphatically, "Even if I have to die with you, I will never disown you." And all the others said the same.

You can't be in a more important moment for the Gospel of Mark than entering the holy city Jerusalem, at the week-long festival of Unleavened Bread and Passover (which overlapped as a single celebration), after having predicted death as a result of opposition to Jesus and his kingdom vision, and after discovering crowds of people who thought Jesus was the ticket to the Age to Come. The long walk from Galilee down the Jordan Valley to Jericho and up to Jerusalem gave Jesus the opportunity to instruct his disciples in order to prepare them for what was to come. They didn't know it, but Jesus knew he would not be with them as they knew his presence.

The Gospel of Mark was written with a tragic ending in view. Even if that tragic crucifixion is overcome by the resurrection, the cross looms over the entire Gospel, at least from John's arrest (1:14) and that escalating opposition to Jesus (2:6–7, 16, 18, 23; 3:1, 6). Once Jesus predicts his own death (8:31), the manner of his death looms over the entire narrative. Today's passage *anticipates* the Cross in three separate events. After these three sections, the arrest unraveling into a crucifixion dominates the Gospel's plot. It is here that we may forget the theme of the Gospel: to follow Jesus means a discipleship shaped by a Jesus of the Cross. To be attached with the Jesus of today's passage is to be attached to a problem in the high places of Jerusalem.

1: ANTICIPATING JESUS' BURIAL

Mark sets the stage in two packed verses about intrigues in Jerusalem, two verses that form a sandwich structure with 14:10–11: (1) a national feast is imminent; (2) the temple authorities lurk behind the scenes to catch Jesus; (3) their plans are to "arrest Jesus secretly and kill him;" (4) they fear a "riot" from the crowds who love Jesus (14:1–2). Meanwhile, out in Bethany Jesus is at the home of Simon the leper (14:3). At that meal a revelation, skipping anything about his death, Jesus' burial is anticipated. This gets the information out of order, but maybe that's the point.

An unnamed woman, who will be memorialized forever without a name (14:9), anoints Jesus' head (14:3). Her act of extravagant devotion, which would not have stood out from "ordinary" treatment of those with high status, draws fire from those who think the expensiveness of the oil could have been sold to aid the poor (14:4–5). Jesus perceives the situation, flips the script from extravagance for someone with status, and reframes it as an act of preparation for his burial beyond death. Following his death his followers will be able to resume care for the poor (14:6–9). There are two other similar descriptions of an anointing in the Gospels, though they do not at all agree on who and where and when (Luke 7:36–50; John 11:2; 12:1–8).

If one is not aware of Mark's love for sandwiching events, the ending of the first section in today's passage could seem like an afterthought. But sandwiching the beginning and the end leads us to read the anointing more tightly with the powers in Jerusalem. The connection between Bethany and Jerusalem is Judas. The connection is betrayal at a price (14:10–11). Emerson Powery offers a potent observation: "While this unnamed female stranger commits this faithful act, Judas—Jesus' own disciple—commits the most faithless act of the story" (Powery, "Mark," 147).

Jesus is the one who will die and be buried; he is the one who will be betrayed. Discipleship takes its path from the path Jesus walked.

2: Anticipating Jesus' Death

Jesus foreknows or Jesus had already organized a location for his last Passover week meal with his disciples. In that last supper, Jesus will stunningly reveal to those at the table that the bread and wine are his body and blood—"poured out for many" (14:24). In the "large room upstairs" Jesus makes three revelations, two of them predictions and one an instruction.

Before we get to those three items, we pause to dip this text into Passover celebrations. Many today explain how the last supper fits beautifully into the modern-day order of a Passover Seder, but the modern Passover Seder was not in its present form in the first century. The first Passover is recorded in Exodus 12–13, and then rehearsed in Deuteronomy 16 (see also Exodus 23:14–17; Joshua 5:10–12). By the time of Jesus the Passover celebration had grown into a more robust ceremony, even if we don't know the precise details. Truth be told, the events of Mark 14:12–25 fit any meal of Passover week. What should stand out is the total absence of lamb at this meal. That's odd because lamb was the center of the Passover meal itself. Instead, Jesus concentrates his words on bread and wine. One more observation about Passover: the theme was *liberation* from enslavement under Pharaoh of Egypt. As a liberation celebration Passover evoked hope for liberation from Rome, which made Jerusalem a tinder box. Rome was especially concerned with Jerusalem at high holidays.

Now to our three considerations. First, Jesus anticipates his death when he predicts one of the disciples betraying him, which elicits court confusion in the room (14:18–21). Readers of Mark have known since Mark 3:19 that Judas was tagged with "who betrayed him." If you have a mind to care about this, these are Mark's words not the reality of the disciples' experience before the actual betrayal. What the disciples learn in the Passover meal is that one of the Twelve, one who is eating with Jesus, even more one who is close enough to dip bread into the bowl with Jesus, will hand him over to the temple authorities who are on the hunt for him. Jesus turns from an instruction to a dire announcement: it is the Son of Man's destiny to die (8:31 has "must") but the one who betrays him skates on the surface of disaster (14:21).

Second, he anticipates his own death when he instructs them to see the bread as his body and the wine as his blood poured out for redemption (14:22–24). In identifying his body and his blood with that Passover bread and wine, Jesus turns the event into an embodied invitation to participate in himself and the imminent death he was about to experience. When the disciples snapped off some bread and when they took a gulp of that wine they were choosing to enter into Jesus and into his death. Eating this bread and drinking this wine, then, becomes a profound act of a discipleship shaped by the Cross.

All we get at first is a "my body" and a "my blood" but something new is heard when he connects "my blood" to "of the covenant" and with "which is poured out for many." One cannot avoid passages like Exodus 24:8; Isaiah 53:12; Jeremiah 31:31; and Zechariah 9:11 when reading these words. At least Jesus couldn't avoid it. Those drenched in Scripture reading would have at least recognized familiarity. Here are those passages:

> Moses then took the blood, sprinkled it on the people and said, "This is the blood of the covenant that the LORD has made with you in accordance with all these words" (Exodus 24:8).

> Therefore I will give him a portion among the great,
>   and he will divide the spoils with the strong,
> because he poured out his life unto death,
>   and was numbered with the transgressors.
> For he bore the sin of many,
>   and made intercession for the transgressors
>   (Isaiah 53:12).

> "The days are coming," declares the LORD,
>   "when I will make a new covenant
> with the people of Israel
>   and with the people of Judah"
>   (Jeremiah 31:31).

As for you, because of the blood of my covenant
with you,
I will free your prisoners from the waterless pit
(Zechariah 9:11).

We could get fancy and begin to explore each of these passages but to do so would take us beyond what was happening in the last supper with the disciples. They surely were stunned by the "my body" and "my blood," and when he invites them to eat and drink bread and wine now reconfigured, they had to know they were entering into a mystery they had never known. They were entering into God's work of redemption at a brand-new level. They were themselves also anticipating Jesus' death. They assumed a discipleship unlike any they could have known.

Third, though we know Mark is recounting their last meal together, it is not until here that the disciples know that (14:25). In saying he will not eat with them again until the kingdom of God arrives is yet another anticipation of his death.

3: ANTICIPATING JESUS' DENIALS

A discipleship shaped by the Cross will almost never be a steady climb to glory. Such a path challenges everyone, so much so that Jesus lays down a post-dinner statement that must have offended the entire group of apostles. For him to have said "You will all fall away" must not have gone well, but he backs it up with a quotation from the prophet Zechariah that anticipates his death and their falling away. Striking a shepherd scatters the sheep. These words rework his three earlier predictions of his death and what he says next repeats his prediction of resurrection: "But after I have risen, I will go ahead of you into Galilee" (14:28). I don't know about you but I wonder how much of this they actually heard. They may still be stuck with his prediction of their all falling away.

Peter jumps to the occasion to make a singular bold prediction himself that he would never cave to the pressure. Discipleship of the cross involves stumbling along the way. Jesus knows and without hesitation fills out his predictions: "Today—yes, tonight—before the rooster crows twice you yourself will disown me three times" (14:30). Confident and clueless all at once Peter re-states his claim and "all the others said the same" (14:31).

What looms over the entire evening are various anticipations of his death. Each of these three events fills in the picture of the plot of the temple authorities. The disciples appear as ones going along knowing they know better while we, the readers, know more than they do. We know Jesus will die a gruesome death, and we know they will scatter, but we learn what they had to learn: to follow the Jesus of the Cross means laying one's life on the line for Jesus.

I can easily fix my attention on "But after I have risen, I will go ahead of you into Galilee" (14:28). Beyond the Cross is the empty tomb, and that too reshapes discipleship with the energy of hope for the kingdom of God.

QUESTIONS FOR REFLECTION AND APPLICATION

1. How does this passage anticipate the cross?

2. What contrast does Mark set up between the woman anointing Jesus and Judas?

3. How does Jesus use the last meal to create a liturgy for his followers?

4. In your tradition, what words of institution are used in celebrating the Lord's Supper/Eucharist?

5. What emotions and thoughts do you have when participating in the liturgical reminder of Jesus' death?

JESUS OF THE CROSS: PAIN

Mark 14:32–52

³² They went to a place called Gethsemane, and Jesus said to his disciples, "Sit here while I pray." ³³ He took Peter, James and John along with him, and he began to be deeply distressed and troubled. ³⁴ "My soul is overwhelmed with sorrow to the point of death," he said to them. "Stay here and keep watch."

³⁵ Going a little farther, he fell to the ground and prayed that if possible the hour might pass from him. ³⁶ "Abba , Father," he said, "everything is possible for you. Take this cup from me. Yet not what I will, but what you will."

³⁷ Then he returned to his disciples and found them sleeping. "Simon," he said to Peter, "are you asleep? Couldn't you keep watch for one hour? ³⁸ Watch and pray so that you will not fall into temptation. The spirit is willing, but the flesh is weak."

³⁹ Once more he went away and prayed the same thing. ⁴⁰ When he came back, he again found them sleeping, because their eyes were heavy. They did not know what to say to him.

⁴¹ Returning the third time, he said to them, "Are you still sleeping and resting? Enough! The hour has come. Look, the Son of Man is delivered into the hands of sinners. ⁴² Rise! Let us go! Here comes my betrayer!"

⁴³ Just as he was speaking, Judas, one of the Twelve, appeared. With him was a crowd armed with swords and clubs, sent from the chief priests, the teachers of the law, and the elders.

⁴⁴ Now the betrayer had arranged a signal with them: "The one I kiss is the man; arrest him and lead him away under guard." ⁴⁵ Going at once to Jesus, Judas said, "Rabbi!" and kissed him. ⁴⁶ The men seized Jesus and arrested him. ⁴⁷ Then one of those standing near drew his sword and struck the servant of the high priest, cutting off his ear.

⁴⁸ "Am I leading a rebellion," said Jesus, "that you have come out with swords and clubs to capture me? ⁴⁹ Every day I was with you, teaching in the temple courts, and you did not arrest me. But the Scriptures must be fulfilled." ⁵⁰ Then everyone deserted him and fled.

⁵¹ A young man, wearing nothing but a linen garment, was following Jesus. When they seized him, ⁵² he fled naked, leaving his garment behind.

In my childhood church we had a picture on the wall of Jesus on his knees praying. Light emanated from his head, and a light from heaven streamed down to Jesus. The image conveyed an anxious Jesus with clenched fists leaning onto a rock surface as he prayed and looked to the Father above. As a child I experienced pain looking into the face of Jesus. He was alone in that picture, utterly alone. But he was not alone, or utterly alone, in the Gospel reading for today. He was with his chosen three: Peter, James, and John (14:33).

Our passage today is about pain because the life of Jesus involved pain of all sorts, beginning with the emotional pain of facing a violent, bloody death.

EMOTIONAL PAIN

You might do to the text above what I have done in my Bible. Underline the words expressing Jesus' pain in verses thirty-three through thirty-six. Jesus was not a stereotypical Stoic facing death with disinterest and not a care in the world. No, his body was trembling with emotions. Jesus is "deeply distressed and troubled." The former term expresses a kind of amazement bordering on alarm, while the second connotes being anxious and discomforted. Then we have Jesus being "overwhelmed with sorrow," which suggests being swamped with grief in the innermost self, even "to the point of death." So he leaves the disciples to pray and he "fell to the ground," which means he collapsed. His prayer to the Father was for his imminent hour of suffering, that is, the Cross itself, could pass him by as its time draws toward him (14:35). He prays, too, that the Cross cup could be taken away from him (14:36). Then he surrenders to the will of the Father.

His pain is palpable, and the wall painting helped me to see that. The words Mark uses make the pain more intense and the emotions of Jesus more real. He did not want to die. He did not want to be crucified in an especially humiliating and family- and disciple-shaming manner. But he wanted even more what the Father wanted. There are no more words for the emotional anxiety and pain of Jesus, but we might just impute them to all three times of prayer recorded in today's passage.

The face of the Cross faces the face of Jesus and the face of Jesus is full of pain. If Jesus reveals the fullness of God, as Paul tells us in Colossians 2 and which I believe to be true, then God is not a painless God but a pain-experiencing God. Tim Gombis rightly states that "God feels more deeply than anyone else the pain of creation and the suffering of his creatures" (Gombis, *Mark*, 511).

RELATIONAL PAIN

Mark deliberately sketches Jesus in a deep contrast with the disciples. They sleep while Jesus faces the Cross. The script changes: as Jesus slept in the boat while the disciples cried out in fear, now they sleep while he faces the ultimate danger. He slept in the sleep of trust, but their sleep is the sleep of failure. Instead of crying out in horror at the prospect of the Cross, they fall—not on their faces in prayer—but asleep. Jesus faces here relational pain from his closest followers.

Jesus prays three times. He returns to where the disciples were three times. They are asleep three times—while Jesus, their Lord, was in pain. Their lack of empathy, their ignorance of the moment, and their failure to perceive what was about to happen all rush to the front for our judgment. Yet, discipleship of the Cross knows failure and Mark has not been afraid to point out the shortfalls of even the closest followers of Jesus. Their sleep counters the painful question and instructive reminder of Jesus: "Couldn't you keep watch for one hour? Watch and pray so that you will not fall into temptation. The spirit is willing, but the flesh is weak" (14:37–38). The word "watch" echoes the same term used in the previous passage about how to live in the midst of divine judgment (13:34, 35, 37). Their inability to watch caused relational pain to Jesus.

BETRAYAL PAIN

Jesus predicted a betrayal by one of the Twelve only a short time earlier (14:18–21). The disciples evidently did not know who it would be, but they now are about to identify the betrayer. Jesus informs them that he, the Son of Man, is about to be "delivered into the hands of sinners" (14:41). The betrayer has arrived (14:42).

The Galilean man who never once lifted a sword nor threatened anyone with violence discovers his betrayer accompanying "a crowd armed with swords and clubs" and they had been chosen for the task by the whole gamut of temple authorities, that is, "the chief priests, the teachers of the law, and the elders" (14:43). The leading men of Jerusalem, who have plotted nabbing him on the sly (11:18; 12:12), have learned from Judas where to find Jesus. He betrays Jesus with the common act of respect, calling Jesus "Rabbi," which means "My master" or "My great one," and the singular act of friendship, a kiss (14:44–45).

Jesus may not be a man of violence, but "one of those standing near" drew a long knife and sliced off the ear of a slave (NIV has "servant") of the high priest. Jesus, in Mark not saying a word about the act of violence just performed, questions why they need such an array of weapons when they could have nabbed him in the temple courts all week as he was teaching. Everyone deserts Jesus at this moment (14:40), a tragic line expressing the challenge of a discipleship of the Cross. It not only means pain, but it means arrests and violence and potential trials and capital sentence.

Mark has a most interesting detail that seems not to matter one bit to the narrative he is working. He tells us of a "young man" wearing "nothing but a linen garment" who was "following Jesus." Those two words describe more than a spectator. They are chosen words for disciples. When they attempt to nab the young man too, his clothes fall off and the man runs away butt naked (14:51–52). Who is the man? Most often scholars guess it is the author of the Gospel, that is, Mark.

BETRAYAL AS A PAINFUL EXPERIENCE

Betrayal is the worst experience. I have friends who have been betrayed by colleagues, and colleagues who have been betrayed by friends. Jesus, even though he knew he would be betrayed, did not escape or shy away from feelings of shame, dishonor, and broken trust. I now rework what I wrote in the volume on Luke's Gospel (McKnight, *Luke*, 340–341). Betrayal assaults the heart and soul of one who trusts. Betrayals suddenly erase intimacies and love and collapse the foundations of relationships. Betrayals destroy the moral fibers of trust. One should never dismiss a betrayal by minimizing the act or the wounds. Betrayals require emotional strength to face, to endure, and to process. Betrayals may be forgiven but regaining trust requires time. Here is an abstract of a technical study of the psychological impact of betrayal:

> Betrayal is the sense of being harmed by the intentional actions or omissions of a trusted person. The most common forms of betrayal are harmful disclosures of confidential information, disloyalty, infidelity, dishonesty. They can be traumatic and cause considerable distress. The effects of betrayal include shock, loss and grief, morbid pre-occupation, damaged self-esteem, self-doubting, anger. Not infrequently they produce life-altering changes. The effects of a catastrophic betrayal are most relevant for anxiety disorders, and OCD and PTSD in particular. Betrayal can cause mental contamination, and the betrayer commonly becomes a source of contamination (S. Rachman, "Betrayal: A Psychological Analysis").

Jesus was betrayed but so too were the other eleven and the various circles of Jesus' followers, not least his mother and brothers. They all *felt* betrayed.

Following Jesus means following a betrayed Lord, and joining him may itself lead to betrayals.

QUESTIONS FOR REFLECTION AND APPLICATION

1. Jesus is sometimes depicted as being peaceful and unemotional. How does this narrative of his pain contradict that understanding of him?

2. How do the close disciples hurt Jesus in this story?

3. How does Judas hurt Jesus in this story?

4. How do you think the other disciples felt about Judas's betrayal?

5. When have you faced betrayal? What helped you survive and heal?

FOR FURTHER READING

Scot McKnight, Everyday Bible Study Series: *Luke*, (Grand Rapids: HarperChristian Resources, 2023).

S. Rachman, "Betrayal: A Psychological Analysis," *Behaviour Research and Therapy* 48.4 (April, 2010): 304–11. @ doi: 10.1016/j.brat.2009 .12.002. Epub 2009 Dec 24. PMID: 20035927.

JESUS OF THE CROSS: FROM AGENT TO AGENT

Mark 14:53–15:20

Agent temple authorities

53 They took Jesus to the high priest, and all the chief priests, the elders and the teachers of the law came together.

54 Peter followed him at a distance, right into the courtyard of the high priest. There he sat with the guards and warmed himself at the fire.

55 The chief priests and the whole Sanhedrin were looking for evidence against Jesus so that they could put him to death, but they did not find any. 56 Many testified falsely against him, but their statements did not agree.

57 Then some stood up and gave this false testimony against him: 58 "We heard him say, 'I will destroy this temple made with human hands and in three days will build another, not made with hands.' " 59 Yet even then their testimony did not agree.

60 Then the high priest stood up before them and asked Jesus, "Are you not going to answer? What is this testimony that these men are bringing against you?" 61 But Jesus remained silent and gave no answer. Again the high priest asked him, "Are you the Messiah, the Son of the Blessed One?"

⁶² *"I am," said Jesus. "And you will see the Son of Man sitting at the right hand of the Mighty One and coming on the clouds of heaven."*

⁶³ *The high priest tore his clothes. "Why do we need any more witnesses?" he asked.* ⁶⁴ *"You have heard the blasphemy. What do you think?"*

They all condemned him as worthy of death.

⁶⁵ *Then some began to spit at him; they blindfolded him, struck him with their fists, and said, "Prophesy!"*

And the guards took him and beat him.

⁶⁶ *While Peter was below in the courtyard, one of the servant girls of the high priest came by.* ⁶⁷ *When she saw Peter warming himself, she looked closely at him.*

"You also were with that Nazarene, Jesus," she said.

⁶⁸ *But he denied it. "I don't know or understand what you're talking about," he said, and went out into the entryway.*

⁶⁹ *When the servant girl saw him there, she said again to those standing around, "This fellow is one of them."* ⁷⁰ *Again he denied it.*

After a little while, those standing near said to Peter, "Surely you are one of them, for you are a Galilean."

⁷¹ *He began to call down curses, and he swore to them, "I don't know this man you're talking about."*

⁷² *Immediately the rooster crowed the second time. Then Peter remembered the word Jesus had spoken to him: "Before the rooster crows twice you will disown me three times." And he broke down and wept.*

Agent Roman governor

¹⁵:¹ *Very early in the morning, the chief priests, with the elders, the teachers of the law and the whole Sanhedrin, made their plans. So they bound Jesus, led him away and handed him over to Pilate.*

² *"Are you the king of the Jews?" asked Pilate.*

"You have said so," Jesus replied.

³ The chief priests accused him of many things. ⁴ So again Pilate asked him, "Aren't you going to answer? See how many things they are accusing you of."

⁵ But Jesus still made no reply, and Pilate was amazed.

⁶ Now it was the custom at the festival to release a prisoner whom the people requested. ⁷ A man called Barabbas was in prison with the insurrectionists who had committed murder in the uprising. ⁸ The crowd came up and asked Pilate to do for them what he usually did.

⁹ "Do you want me to release to you the king of the Jews?" asked Pilate, ¹⁰ knowing it was out of self-interest that the chief priests had handed Jesus over to him. ¹¹ But the chief priests stirred up the crowd to have Pilate release Barabbas instead.

¹² "What shall I do, then, with the one you call the king of the Jews?" Pilate asked them.

¹³ "Crucify him!" they shouted.

¹⁴ "Why? What crime has he committed?" asked Pilate.

But they shouted all the louder, "Crucify him!"

¹⁵ Wanting to satisfy the crowd, Pilate released Barabbas to them. He had Jesus flogged, and handed him over to be crucified.

Agent guards and soldiers

(Cf. 14:65 above.)

¹⁶ The soldiers led Jesus away into the palace (that is, the Praetorium) and called together the whole company of soldiers. ¹⁷ They put a purple robe on him, then twisted together a crown of thorns and set it on him. ¹⁸ And they began to call out to him, "Hail, king of the Jews!" ¹⁹ Again and again they struck him on the head with a staff and spit on him. Falling on their knees, they paid homage to him. ²⁰ And when they had mocked him, they took off the purple robe and put his own clothes on him. Then they led him out to crucify him.

If we look back at this Gospel, we recall that Rome was sovereign over Judea and Galilee. The primary Romans in charge begin in Rome with Tiberius, who surrendered too much power to his own agent, Sejanus. The emperor has an agent in Judea (Pilate) and Galilee (Antipas). These Romans kept their eyes on, and at the same time co-ruled with, the temple authorities in Jerusalem. The temple authorities had received reports about a Galilean movement led by Jesus from Nazareth. To keep their eyes on Jesus so Rome would not need to keep its eyes on the temple authorities, the authorities sent Pharisees and scribes (NIV: "teachers of the law") to Galilee, who at times joined hands with the Herodians, who were agents of Antipas. The tension between Jesus and the Pharisees, and whoever was with the Pharisees, was tension between Jesus and Jerusalem as well as ultimately Jerusalem and Rome. Such a network of relations alone can explain what happens to Jesus and why it happened. All the agents of Rome were in the business of keeping out of trouble by preserving the peace. Jesus was a threat to that peace. Tiberius was the Roman emperor and Suetonius records of Tiberius that "he took great pains to prevent outbreaks of the populace and punished such as occurred with the utmost severity" (Suetonius, *Tiberius*, xxxvii).

In today's passage Jesus is passed from one agent to another. The plot is clear: the temple authorities want the Roman authority to put Jesus away. Discipleship enters into this plot as well in two ways: Peter's denials show the challenge of a faithful witness when under fire, while Jesus' own passing from agent to agent reminds us of what Jesus said would also happen to his gospel witnesses (13:9–13). Which means once again that the life of Jesus forms the paradigm for the life of a follower of Jesus.

AGENT TEMPLE AUTHORITIES

Our first section, which forms into an uneven sandwich about Peter (14:54), uneven because the top piece of bread in this sandwich is very thin with only one verse (15:54) while the lower piece of bread is quite thick (14:66–72). In between these two uneven pieces of the sandwich Mark develops the hearing before the "whole Sanhedrin" (14:53, 55–65). The word trial is often used for what happens in today's passage, but that term may be too technical to describe what happens. The word hearing seems more appropriate. Ordering the passage this way presses upon listeners and readers a stiff warning that sticking up for Jesus in life-threatening moments challenges one's faithfulness. In addition, as Jesus is confronted with a hearing so also is Peter. Plus, the powers judging Jesus are the temple state's leading authorities who are accountable to Rome. One may not excuse Peter, but one should not disrespect the gravity of his challenge either.

The temple authorities at work in the first section include the high priest (Caiaphas), the chief priests, the elders, and the scribes (14:53, 55, 60, 63). Mark sweeps them all into a pile as the "whole Sanhedrin" (14:55). But please notice the absence of Pharisees, and that's because the groups above are the ones with the power. The Pharisees are their agents. Mark seems to impute unjust motives when he says they "were looking for evidence against Jesus so that they could put him to death" (14:55), but we should guard against insinuating too much. I see it as their attempt to put into the legal record what Jesus had been doing, like tipping over tables, teaching, challenging authorities, and predicting in the temple courts (Mark 11–13). Yet, because their evidence was insufficient for the death penalty, they then produce some false testimony (14:56–59). Twice Mark informs us these false witnesses produced conflicting stories (14:56, 59).

When Jesus was asked to respond to his accusers, Jesus turned the dial to silence (14:61a). So the high priest ramps up his interrogation by asking Jesus if he is "the Messiah, the Son of the Blessed One" (14:61b). Jesus responds this time by informing the high priest with two answers: (1) Yes, using the same language in John's Gospel of the I AM sayings, and (2) Caiaphas will someday witness the "Son of Man sitting at the right hand of the Mighty One and coming on the clouds of heaven," which comes from Daniel 7 (cf. 13:26 and 14:62). We must understand Jesus here claiming to be that figure in Daniel, a figure who will be oppressed but vindicated before God. The high priest sure did, which is why he accuses Jesus of blasphemy (14:63–64). So they "all condemned him as worthy of death" and then physically abused the body of Jesus (14:64–65).

Now we get the reason for Mark's placing Peter in the courtyard at the outset of this passage (14:54). Three times Peter is challenged about his relationship with Jesus. Three times Peter denies it. The rooster crows, and Peter wails because he remembers the prediction of Jesus. That memory unleashed shame on Peter's part for not remaining faithful to Jesus when faithfulness was most needed (14:66–72). To follow Jesus means following the real Jesus, not the Jesus we'd like him to be or the celebrity Jesus. The real Jesus was arrested, hauled before a hearing, found worthy of death, and abused physically. No wonder Peter denied association with Jesus. Yet, association embodies the deepest discipleship demand of Jesus (8:34–9:1; 9:33–37; 10:35–45). Like blind Bartimaeus, Peter's own vision of discipleship was murky and he lost his courage in his courtyard hearing.

AGENT ROMAN GOVERNOR

The temple authorities pass Jesus on to the Roman governor, or prefect (who lived at Caesarea Maritima), Pilate because their allegations are insufficient to stick. Pilate seems less convinced than the strong words of Caiaphas in Mark 14:63–64. But even more than Caiaphas, the clamor over Jesus presented by Mark puts Pilate in an even tougher spot than Caiaphas'. Reframing the question of Caiaphas, Pilate does not interrogate Jesus about being Messiah or Son of God. He goes straight to outright mutiny and rebellion by asking if he is the "king of the Jews" (15:2). Jesus only cracks the door open to peek out with less than an answer. Jesus answers "You say." The NIV fills it out with "You have said so" and turns a present tense into a past perfect tense. In light of Jesus' "I am" to Caiaphas this "you say" is far less of an affirmative answer.

The chief priests are present and add to the allegations against Jesus, which leads Pilate to do as Caiaphas had just done. He asked Jesus if he wanted to respond, and as Jesus did before Caiaphas, Jesus had no answer (15:3–5). Pilate was stunned because he had the power of life and death. Jesus shows no desire to save his life. Mark turns to a custom not known from any other Jewish source. A custom of liberating a prisoner at Passover, which if there is no criminal record there's every reason for Jews to have done. Passover was all about liberating the enslaved (15:6). So Pilate raises the name of "Barabbas," which ironically means "Son of the father," which is not a little of an echo of Jesus' own claims of his relationship with God the Father. Contrary to some recorded behaviors of Pilate, who had a reputation for being ruthless, Pilate caves. At the instigation of the leading priests the crowds clamor for a sentence of crucifixion. Pilate seems still less than persuaded but gives in to the crowds lest Rome send in troops to calm things down. He has Jesus flogged to "satisfy the crowd" and "handed him over to be crucified" (15:7–11).

Where's Peter? Add it up, where are any of the apostles? Jesus was alone.

AGENT GUARDS AND SOLDIERS

Jesus was passed from the temple authorities and Caiaphas to Pilate by "guards" who had slapped Jesus to humiliate Jesus publicly (14:65; cf. Matthew 5:39). Mark 14:65's record of a humiliation ceremony forms a sandwich with a bigger event in 15:16–20. Here they form a caravan with Jesus to the palace and gather the entire cohort of soldiers (15:16). The allegation that Jesus claims to be king of the Jews (15:2), now lodged successfully against Jesus by Pilate's judgment, leads soldiers to suit Jesus up in a royal-claiming purple robe and to crown him with a crown, not of gold or diadems but of thorns. Suited up, they mock him and beat him with a reed and a staff and spit at him—all acts done to humiliate him as their scapegoat. They fake obeisance and strip him of the royal robe and reclothe him with his own clothing and lead him out of the Praetorium for the ultimate public humiliation: crucifixion.

Where are Peter and the apostles? Jesus was alone.

From Mark 3:6 on this moment was the plot of the Romans and Jerusalem's temple authorities. Most of the events from those early days in Galilee had been observed by the disciples. They observed how Jesus responded and they were learning what it meant to be attached to a Jesus with such a pattern of life. Their absence, a dismal failure, will be undone by Easter and by a resumption of discipleship. Discipleship includes failure and repentance and confession and returning to the path Jesus himself walked.

QUESTIONS FOR REFLECTION
AND APPLICATION

1. How do the power-mongers relate to each other in Mark? What is the relationship between the key power players?

2. How do those complicated relationships play out in Jesus' hearing?

3. Write in this book and compose parallel columns comparing Jesus before the authorities and Peter before his questioners. What do you notice?

4. Compare Jesus' responses to the authorities with Isaiah 52:13–53:12. What do you notice?

5. Read Mark 13:11 and compare it to how both Jesus and Peter respond to those interrogating them. What do you notice?

FOR FURTHER READING

Suetonius, *Lives of the Caesars.* 2 volumes.
   Volume 1, Book 3: *Tiberius.* Loeb Classical
   Library. Translated by J.C. Rolfe (Cambridge,
   Massachusetts: Harvard University Press, 1998),
   310–417.

JESUS OF THE CROSS: FROM THE PALACE TO THE GRAVE

Mark 15:20b–47

Led

20b Then they led him out to crucify him.

21 A certain man from Cyrene, Simon, the father of Alexander and Rufus, was passing by on his way in from the country, and they forced him to carry the cross. 22 They brought Jesus to the place called Golgotha (which means "the place of the skull"). 23 Then they offered him wine mixed with myrrh, but he did not take it.

Crucified

24 And they crucified him. Dividing up his clothes, they cast lots to see what each would get.

25 It was nine in the morning when they crucified him. 26 The written notice of the charge against him read: THE KING OF THE JEWS.

27 They crucified two rebels with him, one on his right and one on his left. 29 Those who passed by hurled insults at him, shaking their heads and saying, "So! You who are going to destroy the temple and build it in three days, 30 come down from the cross and save yourself!" 31 In the same way the chief priests and the teachers of the law mocked him among themselves. "He saved others," they said, "but he can't save himself! [32] *Let this Messiah, this king of Israel, come down now from the cross, that we may see and believe." Those crucified with him also heaped insults on him.*

Died

[33] *At noon, darkness came over the whole land until three in the afternoon.* [34] *And at three in the afternoon Jesus cried out in a loud voice, "Eloi, Eloi, lema sabachthani?" (which means "My God, my God, why have you forsaken me?").*

[35] *When some of those standing near heard this, they said, "Listen, he's calling Elijah."*

[36] *Someone ran, filled a sponge with wine vinegar, put it on a staff, and offered it to Jesus to drink. "Now leave him alone. Let's see if Elijah comes to take him down," he said.*

[37] *With a loud cry, Jesus breathed his last.*

[38] *The curtain of the temple was torn in two from top to bottom.* [39] *And when the centurion, who stood there in front of Jesus, saw how he died, he said, "Surely this man was the Son of God!"*

[40] *Some women were watching from a distance. Among them were Mary Magdalene, Mary the mother of James the younger and of Joseph, and Salome.* [41] *In Galilee these women had followed him and cared for his needs. Many other women who had come up with him to Jerusalem were also there.*

Buried

[42] *It was Preparation Day (that is, the day before the Sabbath). So as evening approached,* [43] *Joseph of Arimathea, a prominent member of the Council, who was himself waiting for the kingdom of God, went boldly to Pilate and asked for Jesus' body.* [44] *Pilate was surprised to hear that he was already dead. Summoning the centurion, he asked him if Jesus had already died.* [45] *When he learned from the centurion that it was so, he gave the body to Joseph.* [46] *So Joseph bought some linen cloth, took down the body, wrapped it in*

the linen, and placed it in a tomb cut out of rock. Then he rolled a stone against the entrance of the tomb. [47] Mary Magdalene and Mary the mother of Joseph saw where he was laid.

To follow Jesus, the real Jesus, is to walk behind someone who entered Jerusalem to acclaim and was led out of Jerusalem to an ignominious death on a cross. His life and death become the pattern for discipleship. As we read today's passage—and please don't skim it—ponder what the disciples saw. They did not see it all, but some of it they did see even from a distance. Mark paints in deep, dark hues with mere flicks of light a most gruesome scene. Jesus is alone. That scene reveals the "end" of Jesus' life on earth. Its brutality may be masked among many of us, but this summary can bring us back to a social reality: "Since the victim was stripped naked and fixed immobile to suffer the torments of pain, thirst, insults and taunts, sometimes for days, it was particularly humiliating, as well as a prolonged and agonizing form of death" (Hooker, *Mark*, 371). Difficult deaths not only draw the faithful to Jesus, but Jesus is drawn to them in their death.

LED

Jesus was no longer in control of his life. He was at the mercy of the Roman-sponsored soldiers who conscripted an otherwise unknown African man named Simon to carry the cross for Jesus. Simon was the father of Alexander and Rufus, who must have been known to Mark's audience (15:21). Neither Matthew nor Luke include this father-fact.

CRUCIFIED

The location for the morning crucifixion is "the place called the Skull" (Aramaic *Golgotha*, Latin *Calvary*), most likely now under the Church of the Holy Sepulchre. The powerful used the tortures of crucifixion as a deterrent, but their most potent communication was sadism, revenge, brutality, and grisly displays of power. Crucifixions attracted crowds of observers. Crucifixions were more than deterrents, then, since they were also used as revenge to humiliate the victim and anyone attached to the person. The Romans believed such acts of "justice" led to *pax Romana*, and it was the peace that Rome thought was peace. A more accurate term than peace was domination or usurpation.

As a sedative some, probably out of mercy because of the suffering Jesus was about to experience, offered him "wine mixed with myrrh" (15:23). Jesus refuses as he chooses to look death straight in the face. To say "they crucified him" means they fixed the vertical pole and the cross beam into place, with Jesus nailed to both. Jesus suffocated to death. Still alive and in view of Jesus they divide his clothes by casting lots to see who would get what—like it was a prize possession to own the clothing of a crucified man (15:24).

The titulus above him, which records the reason for the crucifixion, returns to the question of Pilate, a question if answered in the affirmative by Jesus would make him officially an insurrectionist and worthy of capital sentence— "THE KING OF THE JEWS" (15:26). The titulus of course is irony at the highest level, but that does not end the taunting of Jesus. Jesus was crucified with two (other) "rebels" (NIV) though the word means more often a thief, like a highway bandit or a seafaring pirate. Regardless, Pilate attaches Jesus to criminals against the state (15:27).

Mark records more mocking, some from those who "passed by," more from the "chief priests and teachers of the law," and even from the soldiers who did the deed of crucifying him. One group accusing him of powerlessness after claiming the powers to rebuild the temple in three days and the other over his capacity to save others but not himself, while the two "rebels" with him "heaped insults on him" (15:28–32).

DEAD

Three hours after his crucifixion another three-hour period begins, a period of darkness "over the whole land" (15:33). At the end of cosmic shade, at 3pm Jesus cries out the most painful words about God in the whole Bible: *"Eloi, Eloi, lema sabachthani?"* which means "My God, my God, why have you forsaken me?" (15:34). The words pierce and haunt. Jesus is utterly alone. He has been deserted by his closest followers. The words offer consolation to the deserted and to the suffering. Jesus is with them. One wonders now if James and John recalled Jesus asking them if they "can drink the cup I drink?" (10:38). Here the cup is full of what Jesus had in mind. Lament is the only proper response because we must face this crucifixion scene as a barbaric injustice. Yet, we must pause also to see God up close in what Tim Gombis calls "God himself" becoming "the God-abandoned one" (Gombis, *Mark*, 554).

Those "standing near" think he's crying out for Elijah and yet another offers him "wine vinegar" on a "sponge" to drink, and then taunts Jesus to deepen the Elijah mystery with "Let's see if Elijah comes to take him down" (15:35–36). Some thought Elijah would return at the end to liberate Israel (cf. 6:14–16; 9:5, 11–13).

He dies, and Mark records two moments: "With a loud cry, Jesus breathed his last" (15:37). Those two moments lead to an interpretation of what just happened without telling us precisely what the interpretation is. The impact of his death requires the reader to rethink the horror of what just happened and see that this was a death that brought a sign of divine judgment in both the darkness (Exodus 10:21–22;

Amos 8:9) and in yet another indication of the coming destruction of the temple (curtain torn). Yet, it opened the way for one man to enter the presence of God. How else do we understand "the curtain of the temple was torn in two from top to bottom" leading a gentile Roman centurion to confess Jesus as the true "Son of God," which again is a term for a king (15:38)? I cannot shake this. A crucifixion is brutality at its worst but this crucifixion undoes the brutality to reveal that our God reveals true kingship and kingdom in the face of the One Crucified. Which is why Mark so emphatically narrates the Gospel's theme of discipleship as following the whole life of Jesus. (And it's not over.)

Discipleship never gets too far from Mark's biography about Jesus. Women are "watching from a distance," the distance indicating a place of safety but watching, distinguishing them from the male disciples of Jesus (15:40). The women, who are Galilean disciples of Jesus, are named: Mary Magdalene, Mary the mother of James the younger and of Joseph, and Salome. They had served Jesus to contribute to his kingdom mission (15:41). Noticeably, Mark adds "many other women" from Galilee "had come up with him to Jerusalem" (15:41). *Because they were there, because they risked their lives by staying close enough to observe what happened, they become the most credible witnesses of Jesus' resurrection.*

BURIED

It was Friday, called "Preparation [for the Sabbath] Day." Deaths on Fridays required a quick burial. At the threshold of evening, a "prominent member of the Council" (Sanhedrin), named Joseph, who was from Arimathea, was a follower of Jesus who was "waiting for the kingdom of God." Unafraid of retaliation from those in power, he "boldly" enters into the presence of Pilate with a request for the body of Jesus so he can bury the body (15:43). Confirmed by a centurion that Jesus had in fact already died Pilate "gave the body to Joseph" (15:44). It was beyond disgraceful to let a body linger so he wants Jesus' body buried. The details of burial procedures follow: (1) he acquired linen cloth; (2) took down the body from the cross; (3) wrapped the body with the linen; (4) laid the body of Jesus "in a tomb cut out of rock;" and (5) rolled a large stone against the tomb to secure it (15:46). Still watching, Mary Magdalene and Mary the mother of Joseph knew where he was buried—making their witnesses credible again.

QUESTIONS FOR REFLECTION AND APPLICATION

1. What was Rome's understanding of peace? Why might it be better understood as domination?

2. What do you think the disciples might have been feeling and thinking as they watched from a distance?

3. What do you observe about the women Mark mentions near the cross?

4. How does their nearness to the cross make them reliable witnesses later?

5. If you had been among the disciples, do you think you could have stood to watch Jesus on the cross?

JESUS OF THE CROSS: SURPRISES AND NO SURPRISE

Mark 16:1–8

¹ When the Sabbath was over, Mary Magdalene, Mary the mother of James, and Salome bought spices so that they might go to anoint Jesus' body. ² Very early on the first day of the week, just after sunrise, they were on their way to the tomb ³ and they asked each other, "Who will roll the stone away from the entrance of the tomb?"

⁴ But when they looked up, they saw that the stone, which was very large, had been rolled away. ⁵ As they entered the tomb, they saw a young man dressed in a white robe sitting on the right side, and they were alarmed.

⁶ "Don't be alarmed," he said. "You are looking for Jesus the Nazarene, who was crucified. He has risen! He is not here. See the place where they laid him. ⁷ But go, tell his disciples and Peter, 'He is going ahead of you into Galilee. There you will see him, just as he told you.' "

⁸ Trembling and bewildered, the women went out and fled from the tomb. They said nothing to anyone, because they were afraid.

This Gospel ends exactly where Jesus told the disciples it would end. Jesus predicted not just his death but his resurrection. The oddity of the ending of Mark, and the printed text above that ends as it does at 16:8, is by far the most reliable ending. Because of where it ends, some later Christians added more material to give the Gospel a happier ending. They preferred Mark to end as do Matthew, Luke, and John. But they are not Mark, and Mark ends where Mark ends.

SURPRISES

Sunday morning is the most important day for the church. But only because three women, two Marys and a Salome, risked themselves to anoint Jesus. The NIV, by adding "the body of" misses the direction of the action. The women are caring for the person. Their concern was how they could dislodge the massive stone from the tomb's opening. To their (first) surprise they observed that "the stone, which was very large, had been rolled away" (16:4). *Wonderful*, they must have immediately said to themselves, but this would have been followed up with *Who did this?* and *Why?* And maybe, *Have they taken Jesus away?*

Not put off enough by such questions they "entered the tomb" and discovered, not Jesus, but "a young man dressed in a white robe" (16:5). That was their second surprise. Mark's term is intense, which is why the NIV has "alarmed" and it suggests being terrified. The third and biggest surprise is next: "He has risen!" (16:6). Jesus had predicted not only his crucifixion but his resurrection, and the young man's word establishes that what he predicted has come to pass. They did not need to be told to leave to inform "the disciples and Peter," but the young man did urge them to do that, but what surprises (fourth) is that Jesus has moved on to Galilee so they will all have to return home to see the risen Lord (16:7; cf. 14:28). They all failed him at his hearings and crucifixion, not least Peter, but Jesus is ready to reconcile with them when they get back to Galilee.

No Surprise

It's not every day, of course, that someone encounters a resurrection. So, I know I am empathic with their responses. "Trembling and bewildered" is how the NIV puts it in the final verse of the Gospel. The Common English Bible has "Overcome with terror and dread," while the NRSVue has "for terror and amazement had seized them." In *The Second Testament* I translate literally with "they had tremble and ecstasy." The word "ecstasy" (or bewildered, dread, amazement) has a sense of seeing something that makes one back off, while it can also denote a person's ecstatic experience or trance. When connected, as it is in today's passage with "tremble" and "afraid," the sense takes on those hues. They have been overcome with something beyond their imagination and experience. They have met the divine, the numinous, the supernatural up close and personal and they have no way to comprehend the incomprehensible.

Instead of telling the disciples, they flop. "They said nothing to anyone" (16:8).

This, too, fits the Gospel of Mark. This experience in the tomb uses words found in the three passion predictions (8:31; 9:31; 10:33). The no-surprise element is that the response of the women is just like Peter's in chapter eight and James and John and the rest of the disciples in chapter ten. Failure to respond to revelations about what God is doing shapes how Mark wants his readers to understand discipleship. It's a journey on which at times followers of Jesus flop and fail and fall off the path. In Mark Jesus often tells those who witnessed some act of God done by Jesus not to tell them, but those told go blab all around. Now that the disciples are told to talk, they go silent. The stupendously good news of Jesus' resurrection has been handed on to three women witnesses of the empty tomb.

Mark ends there.

So do we.

QUESTIONS FOR REFLECTION AND APPLICATION

1. Why do you think Mark ended his Gospel as he did?

2. Why were the disciples surprised when Jesus had actually predicted his resurrection?

3. What do you make of Mark's intense emotional language?

4. What can you do to talk about Jesus and his work and teachings in your world?

5. Now that you have completed this study, who do you say Jesus is?

New Testament
Everyday Bible Study Series

In the **New Testament Everyday Bible Study Series,** widely respected biblical scholar Scot McKnight combines interpretive insights with pastoral wisdom for all the books of the New Testament.

Each volume provides:

- Original Meaning. Brief, precise expositions of the biblical text and offers a clear focus for the central message of each passage.

- Fresh Interpretation. Brings the passage alive with fresh images and what it means to follow King Jesus.

- Practical Application. Biblical connections and questions for reflection and application for each passage.

— AVAILABLE IN THE SERIES —

James and Galatians

Acts

Philippians and 1 & 2 Thessalonians

1 & 2 Timothy, Titus, and Philemon

John

Luke

Romans

Mark

Ⓗ Harper*Christian* Resources

The Blue Parakeet, 2nd Edition

Rethinking How You Read the Bible

Scot McKnight, author of
The Jesus Creed

How are we to live out the Bible today? In this updated edition of *The Blue Parakeet*, you'll be challenged to see how Scripture transcends culture and time, and you'll learn how to come to God's Word with a fresh heart and mind.

The gospel is designed to be relevant in every culture, in every age, in every language. It's fully capable of this, and, as we read Scripture, we are called to discern how God is speaking to us today.

And yet applying its words and directions on how to live our lives is not as easy as it seems. As we talk to the Christians around us about issues that matter, many of us wonder: how on earth are we reading the same Bible? How is it that two of us can sit down with the same Bible and come away with two entirely different answers about everything from charismatic gifts to the ordaining of women?

Professor and author of *The King Jesus Gospel* Scot McKnight challenges us to rethink how to read the Bible, not just to puzzle it together into some systematic belief or historical tradition but to see it as an ongoing Story that we're summoned to enter and to carry forward in our day.

What we need is a fresh blowing of God's Spirit on our culture, in our day, and in our ways. We need twenty-first-century Christians living out the biblical gospel in twenty-first-century ways. And if we read the Bible properly, we will see that God never asked one generation to step back in time and live in ways of the past.

Through the Bible, God speaks in each generation, in that generation's ways and beckons us to be a part of his amazing story.

Available in stores and online!